I0522252

BRANDEE JANKOSKI
KEVIN GLYNN

Smoke and Sizzle

Mastering the Art of Smoking and Grilling
Complete How-To Guide for Flavorful Outdoor
Cooking with Easy to Make Recipes

Contents

8. Conclusion

9. Thank You

Introduction

Welcome to "Smoke and Sizzle: Mastering the Art of Grilling and Smoking!"

In this culinary journey, we embark on a flavorful adventure that celebrates the time-honored traditions of grilling and smoking. Whether you're a seasoned pitmaster looking to refine your skills or a novice eager to explore the world of outdoor cooking, this cookbook is your comprehensive guide to achieving that perfect balance of smoky goodness and sizzling perfection.

Purpose of the Cookbook

The purpose of "Smoke and Sizzle" is to unlock the secrets and techniques behind grilling and smoking that have delighted taste buds for centuries. Through the pages of this cookbook, we aim to empower you with the knowledge and skills needed to become a true grilling and smoking aficionado. From juicy steaks and tender ribs to succulent vegetables and mouthwa- tering desserts, you'll discover an array of recipes that will take your outdoor cooking prowess to the next level. Whether you're craving the simplicity of a classic burger or the complexity of a slow-smoked brisket, this cookbook will be your go-to resource for achieving culinary excellence in your own backyard.

Overview of Grilling vs. Smoking

Grilling and smoking may seem similar on the surface, but they each offer unique flavors, techniques, and experiences. In this cookbook, we'll provide a comprehensive overview of these two distinct cooking methods. Grilling is all about high heat, quick cooking, and achieving those beautiful sear marks on your food, while smoking involves slow cooking at lower temperatures with the addition of wood smoke to infuse a deep, smoky flavor. We'll delve into the equipment, fuel sources, and fundamental principles behind both grilling and smoking, helping you make informed decisions on which method to choose for your culinary creations.

Prepare to embark on a culinary adventure that will ignite your passion for outdoor cooking and elevate your culinary skills. "Smoke and Sizzle" is not just a cookbook; it's your gateway to becoming a true grill master and pitmaster extraordinaire. Get ready to fire up the grill, stoke the smoker, and savor the incredible flavors that await you in the world of grilling and smoking.

Essentials of Grilling and Smoking

Types of Grills and Smokers

Choosing the right grill or smoker is a crucial step in your journey to becoming a grill and smoke master. Each type of equipment offers a unique cooking experience, and understand- ing their characteristics will help you make an informed choice based on your preferences and cooking goals. In this section, we'll explore the various types of grills and smokers available to you:

Grills

1. Charcoal Grills:

- Flavor and Aroma: Charcoal grills are renowned for impart- ing a smoky flavor and a mouthwatering aroma to your food.
- Cooking Method: These grills rely on charcoal briquettes or lump charcoal as the heat source. You'll learn the art of creating two-zone cooking, direct and indirect grilling, and achieving the perfect sear.
- Control and Skill: Charcoal grilling requires practice to control temperature and manage the coals effectively.

2. Gas Grills:

- Flavor and Convenience: Gas grills are known for their convenience, quick heat-up times, and ease of use.
- Cooking Method: These grills use propane or natural gas as a heat source and offer precise temperature control. We'll explore techniques for infusing smoky flavors using wood chips or smoker boxes.
- Control and Versatility: Gas grills provide precise temperature control, making them versatile for various cooking styles and dishes.

3. Electric Grills:

- Indoor and Small-Space Cooking: Electric grills are perfect for indoor or limited outdoor spaces where open flames or gas may not be practical.
- Cooking Method: Electric grills use electricity to generate heat and are straightforward to operate. You'll discover how to mimic the outdoor grilling experience indoors.
- Clean and Simple: Electric grills are known for their ease of use and minimal cleanup.

Smokers

4. Offset Smokers:

- Traditional Smoking: Offset smokers are the go-to choice for traditionalists who seek low and slow smoking with a genuine wood flavor.

- Cooking Method: These smokers consist of a separate firebox adjacent to the cooking chamber. You'll learn about fire management, wood selection, and maintaining a consistent temperature.

- Flavor and Skill: Offset smokers offer the opportunity to master the art of slow smoking and creating deeply flavored, tender meats.

5. Vertical Water Smokers:

- Moisture and Flavor: Vertical water smokers use a water pan to regulate temperature and moisture, resulting in tender, flavorful meats.

- Cooking Method: Explore the ins and outs of vertical water smoking techniques, including how to control the cooking environment and achieve consistent results.

- Great for Beginners: These smokers are beginner-friendly and offer a forgiving cooking experience.

6. Pellet Smokers:

- Automation and Convenience: Pellet smokers automate tem-perature control and wood pellet feeding, making them user-friendly.

- Cooking Method: Learn how to use wood pellets to add distinct flavors to your smoked creations and enjoy precise temperature control.

- Set and Forget: Pellet smokers allow you to set your desired temperature and let the smoker do the work, making them suitable for both beginners and experienced pitmasters.

Understanding the characteristics and advantages of these various types of grills and smokers will help you choose the right equipment for your culinary aspirations. Whether you're drawn to the rich flavors of charcoal, the convenience of gas, or the slow-smoking tradition of offset smokers, you're now equipped with the knowledge to make an informed decision. Each type offers its own unique experience, allowing you to tailor your outdoor cooking adventures to your personal preferences and culinary goals.

Tools and Accessories

To become a grill and smoke master, it's essential to have the right tools and accessories in your outdoor cooking arsenal. These tools will not only make your cooking experience more efficient but also help you achieve the best possible results. In this section, we'll discuss the essential items you should have on hand:

1. Grill Grates and Grilling Baskets:

-   Grill Grates: The grates on your grill play a pivotal role in cooking. Stainless steel or cast iron grates are excellent choices. They provide even heat distribution, create beautiful grill marks, and are easy to clean. Ensure your grates are well-maintained, seasoned, and cleaned after each use.
-   Grilling Baskets: Grilling delicate or small items like fish, vegetables, or shrimp can be tricky. Grilling baskets are designed to hold these items securely, making it easier to flip and prevent them from falling through the grates. They come in various shapes and sizes, catering to different ingredients.

2. Thermometers:

-   Instant-Read Thermometer: An instant-read ther- mometer is a must-have tool for grilling and smoking. It ensures that your meats are cooked to the desired level of doneness, preventing overcooking or undercooking. Insert the probe into the thickest part of the meat for accurate readings.
-   Wireless Meat Thermometer: For longer cooking ses- sions, such as smoking a brisket or a whole turkey, a wireless meat thermometer with remote monitoring ca- pabilities can be a game-changer. It allows you to keep an eye on the temperature without constantly opening the grill or smoker. (We recommend Meater at Meater.com)

3. Tongs, Spatulas, and Brushes:

-   Tongs: A good pair of long-handled tongs is essential for flipping, turning, and maneuvering food on the grill. Look for tongs with a locking mechanism for easy storage.
-   Spatulas: Spatulas are ideal for flipping burgers, fish, and other delicate items. They come in various shapes and sizes, so choose one that suits your needs.
-   Basting Brushes: Basting brushes are indispensable for applying marinades, sauces, or oil to your food while grilling or smoking. Silicone brushes are easy to clean and maintain.

4. Wood Chips and Chunks:

-   Wood Chips: Wood chips are essential for adding smoky flavor to your grilled and smoked dishes. Different woods impart distinct flavors, so experiment with varieties like hickory, mesquite, apple, or cherry to enhance your dishes.
-   Wood Chunks: Larger wood chunks are ideal for long smoking sessions. They smolder more slowly, providing a steady release of smoke flavor. Soak them in water before use to create a longer-lasting smoke source.

5. Smoke Boxes and Pellet Tubes:

-   Smoke Boxes: If you're using a gas grill and want to add smoky flavor, smoke boxes are a valuable tool. They hold wood chips or chunks and sit directly on the grill grates, allowing the wood to smolder and infuse your food with smoky goodness.

- Pellet Tubes: For additional smoke flavor on a gas grill or smoker, pellet tubes are a great choice. Fill them with wood pellets and place them on the grill grates, and they will smolder, providing continuous smoke during your cook.

Having these tools and accessories in your outdoor cooking arsenal will not only make your grilling and smoking ses- sions more enjoyable but also enhance your ability to create delicious, flavorful dishes. As you progress in your journey to becoming a grill and smoke master, you may discover additional tools and gadgets that suit your cooking style and preferences. Remember that proper maintenance and care of your tools are essential for their longevity and continued performance, so keep them clean and in good condition to ensure successful cooking adventures.

Safety Tips and Maintenance

Grilling and smoking are not just about creating delicious dishes; they also require responsible practices to ensure safety for you, your family, and your guests. In this section, we'll provide essential safety tips and maintenance guidelines to help you enjoy incident-free outdoor cooking adventures.

Fire Safety:

1. Location: Choose a suitable location for your grill or smoker. Ensure it's placed on a stable, non-combustible surface, away from flammable materials like overhang- ing branches, dry leaves, and wooden structures.

2. Clearance: Maintain a safe distance between your grill or smoker and any nearby objects. Keep a minimum of 10 feet of clearance from your house or other structures to prevent fire hazards.

3. Fire Extinguisher: Have a fire extinguisher nearby and know how to use it. Grease fires can happen, so being prepared is essential.

4. Children and Pets: Keep children and pets away from the grilling or smoking area. Establish a safe zone to prevent accidents.

Food Safety:

1. Hand Washing: Always wash your hands thoroughly before and after handling raw meat or other ingredients to prevent cross-contamination.

2. Marinating: Marinate food in the refrigerator, not at room temperature. Discard any leftover marinade that has come into contact with raw meat.

3. Safe Internal Temperatures: Use a meat thermometer to ensure meats reach safe internal temperatures:

- Poultry: 165°F (74°C)

- Pork and ground meat: 160°F (71°C)

- Fish: 145°F (63°C)

- Steaks, roasts, and seafood: 145°F (63°C)

4. Resting: Allow cooked meats to rest before serving. This helps juices redistribute, ensuring a juicy, flavorful result.

Maintenance:

1. Regular Cleaning: Clean your grill or smoker after each use. Remove food residue and grease buildup to prevent flare-ups and maintain optimal cooking conditions.

2. Check for Gas Leaks: If you're using a gas grill, regularly inspect the gas lines and connections for leaks. Apply a soapy water solution to joints and connectors, and look for bubbles when the gas is on. If you detect a leak, turn off the gas immediately and repair it before use.

3. Empty Ashes: If you're using a charcoal grill or smoker, empty ashes from the firebox and ash pan after each use. Accumulated ashes can restrict airflow and affect temperature control.

4. Replace Worn Parts: Inspect your grill or smoker for worn-out or damaged parts, such as rusted grates, loose handles, or worn-out gaskets. Replace or repair these parts to ensure safe and effective cooking.

5. Ventilation: Ensure proper ventilation when using your smoker. Adequate airflow is essential for temperature control and preventing the buildup of harmful smoke byproducts.

6. Storage: When not in use, cover your grill or smoker with a weatherproof cover to protect it from the elements. Store propane tanks away from direct sunlight and extreme heat.

By following these safety tips and maintenance guidelines, you'll not only enjoy your grilling and smoking adventures to the fullest but also ensure a safe environment for everyone involved. Remember that safety should always come first, and responsible practices will enhance your cooking experience and the longevity of your equipment. Happy grilling and smoking!

Understanding Ingredients

Meat Selection and Preparation

One of the keys to grilling and smoking success is choosing the right meats and preparing them properly. Each type of meat has its unique characteristics, flavors, and considerations. In this section, we'll explore how to select and prepare different meats, including beef, pork, poultry, and fish, to ensure that your grilled and smoked dishes are nothing short of perfection.

Beef
Selection:

1. Cuts: When it comes to beef, you have a wide variety of cuts to choose from. For grilling, popular choices include ribeye, sirloin, New York strip, and filet mignon. For smoking, cuts like brisket, chuck roast, and short ribs work exceptionally well.

2. Marbling: Look for cuts with good marbling—those fine streaks of fat within the meat. Marbling adds flavor and tenderness to the meat. Prime-grade beef typically has the most marbling.

Preparation:

1. Trimming: Before grilling or smoking, trim excess fat and silverskin from the meat. Leave a thin layer of fat to enhance flavor and moisture.

2. Seasoning: Season the beef with your choice of rub or marinade, ensuring that it complements the cut's natural flavor. Common seasonings include salt, pepper, garlic, and various herbs and spices.

3. Resting: Allow the beef to come to room temperature for about 30 minutes before cooking. This ensures more even cooking.

Pork
Selection:

1. Cuts: Pork offers a wide range of cuts suitable for grilling and smoking. Pork chops, tenderloin, and ribs are popular for grilling, while pork shoulder (butt) and ribs excel in the smoker.

2. Fat Content: Look for cuts with a moderate amount of fat. Fat adds flavor and juiciness to the meat, especially when smoking.

Preparation:

1. Brining: Brining pork, especially lean cuts like chops and tenderloin, can help keep the meat moist and tender. A basic brine includes water, salt, and sugar.

2. Dry Rubs: Season pork with a dry rub composed of spices and herbs. Common ingredients include paprika, cumin, brown sugar, and garlic powder.

3. Indirect Heat: For thicker cuts, use indirect heat on the grill or smoker to ensure even cooking without burning the exterior.

Poultry
Selection:

1. Cuts: Chicken and turkey are popular choices for grilling and smoking. You can use whole birds, wings, thighs, or drumsticks. For smoking, consider whole birds or larger cuts like turkey breast or whole chicken.

2. Skin-On vs. Skinless: Skin-on poultry helps retain moisture and adds flavor, while skinless options are leaner. Choose based on your preference.

Preparation:

1. Marinating: Poultry benefits from marination to en- hance flavor and tenderness. Marinades can include citrus, herbs, and olive oil.

2. Brining: For a juicy and flavorful result, brine poultry before smoking. A basic brine consists of water, salt, sugar, and aromatics like garlic and herbs.

3. Internal Temperature: Poultry must be cooked to a safe internal temperature of 165°F (74°C) to ensure it's fully cooked and safe to eat.

Fish
Selection:

1. Types: Fish like salmon, trout, tilapia, and catfish are excellent choices for grilling and smoking. Opt for fresh, firm fillets or whole fish.

2. Skin: Keeping the skin on fish fillets helps prevent sticking to the grill grates and adds a protective layer during smoking.

Preparation:

1. Marinades: Fish can be marinated in citrus-based mari- nades with herbs and olive oil to enhance flavor.

2. Wood Selection: When smoking fish, use milder woods like cedar, alder, or fruitwoods to complement the deli- cate flavor of the fish.

3. Grilling Baskets: Consider using a grilling basket for whole fish to prevent them from falling apart on the grill.

Understanding the characteristics and best practices for se- lecting and preparing different types of meat is essential for achie- ving outstanding results in your grilling and smoking endeavors. Experiment with various cuts, seasonings, and cooking techniques to find your favorite combinations and create mouthwatering dishes that will impress your family and friends.

Vegetables and Fruits for Grilling

While meats take the center stage in grilling and smoking, vegetables and fruits can play equally vital roles in creating delicious, balanced meals. Grilling vegetables and fruits can elevate your culinary repertoire, providing vibrant colors, flavors, and textures to your dishes. In this section, we'll explore the selection, preparation, and techniques for grilling vegetables and fruits to perfection.

Selecting the Right Vegetables and Fruits

Choosing the right vegetables and fruits is essential for successful grilling. Here are some tips on selecting the best produce:

For Vegetables:

1. Firmness: Opt for firm vegetables with minimal bruising or blemishes. They should be fresh and crisp to ensure they hold up well on the grill.

2. Grilling Varieties: Certain vegetables are well-suited for grilling. Consider bell peppers, zucchini, eggplant, asparagus, portobello mushrooms, and corn on the cob for their excellent grilling characteristics.

3. Size Matters: Cut vegetables into uniform sizes to ensure even cooking. Smaller pieces can be skewered for kebabs, while larger ones can be grilled directly.

For Fruits:

1. Ripeness: Select ripe but firm fruits. They should yield slightly to gentle pressure without being overly soft.

2. Grilling-Friendly Fruits: Fruits like peaches, plums, pineapples, watermelon, and even citrus halves are fantastic for grilling. Their natural sugars caramelize beautifully over the heat.

3. Halves or Slices: Halve or slice fruits as needed for grilling. Larger fruits like pineapples may be cut into rings or wedges, while smaller fruits like strawberries can be grilled whole.

Preparing Vegetables and Fruits

Proper preparation ensures that your vegetables and fruits are ready to take on the grill's heat. Here are some preparation tips:

For Vegetables:

1. Cleaning: Wash vegetables thoroughly and pat them dry before grilling.

2. Marinades or Seasonings: Toss vegetables in olive oil and seasonings such as salt, pepper, garlic, and herbs. Marinades with balsamic vinegar or soy sauce can add flavor depth.

3. Skewering: Use skewers for smaller vegetables like cherry tomatoes, mushrooms, or cubed bell peppers to make them easier to handle on the grill.

For Fruits:

1. Halving or Slicing: Cut fruits into halves, slices, or wedges as needed. Removing pits or seeds from fruits like peaches or avocados is essential.

2. Brushing with Oil: Lightly brush fruits with oil to prevent sticking and enhance caramelization.

3. Sweeteners: Consider adding a touch of sweetness with honey, maple syrup, or brown sugar for a delightful contrast to the smoky grill flavor.

Grilling Techniques

Grilling vegetables and fruits requires specific techniques to achieve the desired results:

- Direct Heat: Preheat your grill to medium-high heat. Place vegetables or fruits directly on the grill grates for a quick sear. Use this method for vegetables like asparagus and thin slices of fruits.

- Indirect Heat: For thicker vegetables like potatoes or denser fruits like pineapple, use indirect heat. Move them away from the direct flames and close the grill lid. This method ensures thorough cooking without burning.

- Grilling Baskets: Grilling baskets or trays with perforations are handy for delicate items like small tomatoes or sliced peppers. They prevent pieces from falling through the grates. Skewering: Skewers work well for vegetables and fruits, allowing you to grill multiple items together. Soak wooden skewers in water before grilling to prevent burning.

- Grill Marks: To achieve appealing grill marks, avoid con- stant flipping. Let vegetables and fruits sit undisturbed on the grill for a few minutes before turning.

- Doneness: Cook vegetables until they are tender and slightly charred. Fruits should caramelize and soften. The exact cooking time varies depending on the item's size and thickness.

- Herbs and Garnishes: Enhance the flavors by adding fresh herbs, a squeeze of citrus, or a sprinkle of cheese after grilling. By understanding the selection, preparation, and grilling techniques for vegetables and fruits, you can incorporate these versatile ingredients into your outdoor cooking reper- toire. Grilled vegetables and fruits not only provide a healthy and colorful accompaniment to your grilled meats but also shine as standalone dishes or creative sides that will impress your guests.

Marinades, Rubs, and Sauces

Marinades, rubs, and sauces are essential elements of outdoor cooking that can transform ordinary ingredients into extraor- dinary dishes. They are the flavor-packed secret ingredients that can take your grilling and smoking adventures to the next level. In this section, we'll delve into the nuances of each and explore how they can be used to elevate your culinary creations.

Marinades

Purpose: Marinades are flavorful liquid mixtures that are used to tenderize and infuse meats, poultry, seafood, or vegetables with flavor. They not only add taste but also help to keep the protein moist during cooking.

Components:

1. Acid: Typically, marinades contain acidic components like vinegar, citrus juice (lemon, lime, or orange), yogurt, or wine. The acid helps break down muscle fibers, making the meat more tender.

2. Oil: Olive oil, vegetable oil, or other fats are added to the marinade to prevent the meat from sticking to the grill, as well as to carry and distribute flavors.

3. Flavorings: Marinades often include aromatic ingredi- ents like garlic, herbs, spices, and aromatics such as onions, shallots, and ginger.

4. Sweeteners: Some marinades contain sweeteners like honey, maple syrup, or brown sugar to balance the acidity and add a touch of sweetness.

Usage:

- Marinade times vary depending on the type of protein. Delicate seafood may require only 15-30 minutes, while tougher cuts of meat like beef brisket or pork shoulder can benefit from overnight marinating.

- Always marinate in the refrigerator to prevent food safety concerns.

- Discard used marinades, as they may contain raw meat juices.

Rubs

Purpose: Rubs are dry mixtures of herbs, spices, and sea- sonings applied to the surface of meats, poultry, seafood, or vegetables. They create a flavorful crust and enhance the appearance of the grilled or smoked dish.

Components:

1. Spices: The heart of a rub, spices provide the primary flavor profile. Common ingredients include paprika, chili powder, cumin, coriander, and black pepper.

2. Herbs: Fresh or dried herbs like rosemary, thyme, oregano, and basil add depth and aroma to the rub.

3. Salt: Salt is a crucial component that enhances the flavor of the protein and helps form a crust.

4. Sweeteners: Sugar or brown sugar can be added to balance the spice and provide a caramelized exterior.

Usage:

- Rubs are applied directly onto the surface of the food and should adhere with the help of oil or mustard.
- They are typically used for shorter marinating times or applied just before grilling or smoking.
- Rubs can be used on their own or in combination with marinades for layered flavors.

Sauces

Purpose: Sauces are liquid or semi-liquid condiments that are drizzled, brushed, or served alongside grilled or smoked dishes to add moisture, flavor, and a finishing touch.

Components:

1. Base: Sauces often have a base ingredient, such as tomato sauce, vinegar, mayonnaise, yogurt, or even fruit puree.
2. Flavorings: These include spices, herbs, garlic, onions, and other aromatics. Some sauces may incorporate sweeteners like honey, molasses, or sugar.
3. Acid: Many sauces contain a level of acidity from ingre- dients like citrus juice, vinegar, or wine, which brightens the flavor profile.

Usage:

- Sauces can be used as marinades before grilling, brushed on during cooking for basting, or served as a condiment at the table.
- Some sauces are best applied at the end of cooking to prevent burning or caramelization, while others can withstand higher heat.

Pairing Marinades, Rubs, and Sauces

- Complementary Flavors: Consider the flavors in your marinade, rub, and sauce to ensure they complement each other and the protein you're cooking. For instance, a citrusy marinade pairs well with a tangy barbecue sauce.
- Balancing Act: Be mindful of the balance between sweet, salty, spicy, and acidic elements in your preparations.
- Experimentation: Don't be afraid to experiment with dif- ferent combinations to create your unique flavor profiles.

Understanding the art of marinades, rubs, and sauces opens up a world of culinary creativity in the realm of grilling and smoking. By mastering these essential elements, you can craft dishes that are not only delicious but also customized to your taste preferences, making your outdoor cooking adventures even more rewarding.

Grilling Techniques

Direct vs. Indirect Grilling

Grilling is more than just placing food over an open flame; it involves mastering various techniques to achieve the desired results. Two fundamental grilling techniques you should become familiar with are direct grilling and indirect grilling. Understanding when and how to use each method will help you cook a wide range of dishes to perfection.

Direct Grilling

Definition: Direct grilling is the classic method where food is placed directly over the heat source, such as flames or hot charcoal. It is best suited for cooking small, thin cuts of meat, poultry, seafood, vegetables, and fruits that can be quickly cooked over high heat.

Key Characteristics:

1. 1.　　　High Heat: Direct grilling provides intense, direct heat that sears the exterior of the food, creating appealing grill marks and caramelization.
2. Quick Cooking: This method is ideal for foods that cook in a relatively short time, typically under 20 minutes. Examples include burgers, steaks, hot dogs, and kebabs.
3. Frequent Flipping: You'll need to flip the food regularly to ensure even cooking and prevent burning.

Steps for Direct Grilling:

1. Preheat the Grill: Ensure the grill grates are clean and preheat the grill to the desired high temperature.
2. Oil the Grates: Use a paper towel or grill brush to lightly oil the grates to prevent sticking.
3. Place Food Over the Heat: Arrange the food directly over the heat source on the hot grill grates.
4. Monitor Closely: Keep a close eye on the food and flip it as needed to cook evenly.
5. Adjust Heat: If the food is cooking too quickly or flames are flaring up, you can move it to a cooler part of the grill temporarily or reduce the heat.

Indirect Grilling

Definition: Indirect grilling involves cooking food away from the direct heat source. It's a method typically used for larger cuts of meat, poultry, and dishes that require longer cooking times. Indirect grilling creates an oven-like environment inside the grill, allowing for slow and even cooking without direct flame contact.

Key Characteristics:

1. Low and Slow: Indirect grilling is perfect for achieving low and slow cooking, which is essential for tenderizing tougher cuts of meat and infusing them with smoky flavors.
2. Indirect Heat Source: The heat source, such as a firebox, is separate from the cooking chamber. Heat circulates around the food, creating a convection effect.
3. Longer Cooking Times: Foods that benefit from indirect grilling include whole chickens, pork ribs, roasts, and large cuts like brisket or turkey, which can take hours to cook.

Steps for Indirect Grilling:

1. Preheat the Grill: Preheat only one side of the grill, leaving the other side unlit or set to a lower temperature. If using charcoal, bank the coals to one side.

2. Oil the Grates: Lightly oil the grates on the side where you'll be placing the food.

3. Place a Drip Pan: If desired, place a drip pan filled with water, beer, or other flavorful liquids under the grates on the indirect side. This adds moisture and helps regulate temperature.

4. Position the Food: Place the food on the side of the grill without direct heat. If using a charcoal grill, ensure the food is not directly above the coals.

5. Close the Lid: Keep the grill lid closed to create a consistent cooking environment. Use a thermometer to monitor the temperature inside the grill.

6. Rotate as Needed: Rotate the food occasionally for even cooking. Baste or apply sauces if desired.

By mastering both direct and indirect grilling techniques, you'll have the flexibility to cook a wide variety of dishes, from quick-cooking steaks and burgers to slow-smoked ribs and roasts. Understanding when to use each method is key to achieving delicious, perfectly cooked results on your grill or smoker.

Temperature Control

Temperature control is a fundamental skill in grilling and smoking. It's the key to achieving perfectly cooked dishes, whether you're searing a steak, smoking a brisket, or grilling delicate vegetables. In this section, we'll explore temperature control techniques, including how to manage and adjust heat on your grill or smoker to meet your cooking goals.

The Importance of Temperature Control

Controlling the temperature on your grill or smoker is crucial because different dishes and cuts of meat require specific heat levels and cooking times to achieve the desired results:

- High Heat ($350°F$ to $550°F$): Ideal for searing steaks, burgers, and thin cuts of meat. This high heat creates a flavorful sear on the exterior while retaining a juicy interior.

- Medium Heat ($250°F$ to $350°F$): Suitable for grilling chicken, pork chops, and larger cuts of meat. It allows for thorough cooking without excessive charring.

- Low Heat ($150°F$ to $250°F$): Perfect for smoking, slow- roasting, and cooking tougher cuts of meat. This temper- ature range infuses smoky flavor and tenderizes the meat over an extended period.

Temperature Control Techniques

1. Preheating: Always preheat your grill or smoker before cooking. This ensures that the cooking grates and cooking chamber reach the desired temperature. Allow sufficient time for the grill to stabilize at the chosen heat level.

2. Zone Cooking: Create different heat zones on your grill by arranging the coals or burners accordingly. For a two- zone setup, have one side with high heat (direct heat) and the other with no or low heat (indirect heat). This allows you to move food between zones for different cooking stages.

3. Lid Control: The grill or smoker's lid plays a significant role in temperature control. Closing the lid traps heat and creates an oven-like environment, ideal for indirect grilling or smoking. Opening the lid allows for direct grilling and higher temperatures.

4. Adjustable Vents: Many grills and smokers have ad- justable vents or dampers that control airflow. The intake damper controls the amount of oxygen entering the fire, while the exhaust damper releases smoke and heat. Adjust these dampers to regulate temperature and airflow.

5. Thermometers: Use a grill or meat thermometer to monitor the internal temperature of your grill or smoker. Some models come with built-in thermometers, while others may require an external thermometer probe. Place the probe at the cooking grate level to get an accurate reading of the cooking temperature.

6. Fuel Management: For charcoal grills and smokers, control temperature by adding or reducing the amount of charcoal and adjusting the positioning of the coals. For gas grills, adjust the burner knobs to control heat levels.

Maintaining Temperature Consistency

Maintaining a consistent cooking temperature is essential for achieving reliable and repeatable results. Here are some tips for temperature consistency:

- Avoid Frequent Lid Opening: Every time you open the lid, you release heat and disrupt the cooking environment. Limit lid openings to check food progress or make neces- sary adjustments.

- Fuel Monitoring: Keep an eye on your fuel source, whether it's charcoal, wood, or gas. Add more fuel as needed to maintain the desired temperature.

- Wind Protection: Wind can affect temperature control. Position your grill or smoker in a sheltered location or use windbreaks to minimize its impact.

- Practice: Temperature control is a skill that improves with practice. Experiment with different settings and techniques to understand how your specific grill or smoker behaves.

Temperature control is the backbone of successful grilling and smoking. Whether you're aiming for high-heat searing, slow-smoking, or anything in between, mastering these techniques will empower you to create mouthwatering dishes that consistently impress your family and friends.

Timing and Flipping Techniques

Timing and flipping are crucial aspects of grilling that can make the difference between perfectly cooked dishes and overcooked or undercooked ones. Understanding when and how to flip your food, as well as how long to cook it, is essential for achieving the desired results on your grill. In this section, we'll delve into the techniques of timing and flipping to help you become a grilling maestro.

Timing Techniques

Timing is essential when grilling to ensure that your food cooks evenly and to the desired level of doneness. Here are some timing techniques to keep in mind:

1. Preheat the Grill: Always preheat your grill to the desired cooking temperature before placing food on the grates. This ensures consistent cooking from the start.

2. Use a Timer: While grilling, use a timer to keep track of cooking times. This is especially important for foods that require precise timing, such as thin cuts of meat or delicate vegetables.

3. Consider Food Thickness: The thickness of the food plays a significant role in cooking time. Thicker cuts require more time, while thinner cuts cook faster. Adjust your cooking times accordingly.

4. Flip at the Right Time: Flip your food at the halfway point of the recommended cooking time. This ensures even cooking on both sides.

5. Check for Doneness: Use a meat thermometer to check the internal temperature of meats, poultry, and fish. This is the most accurate way to determine doneness. Reference safe internal temperatures for various foods to ensure they're cooked safely.

6. Resting Period: After grilling, allow meats to rest for a few minutes before cutting or serving. This allows juices to redistribute, resulting in a juicier and more flavorful dish.

Flipping Techniques

Flipping your food properly is essential to achieve grill marks, even cooking, and appealing presentation. Here are some flipping techniques to follow:

1. Use the Right Tools: Invest in a good pair of long-handled tongs or a spatula designed for grilling. These tools allow you to handle food with precision and avoid burns.

2. Flipping Frequency: Avoid constant flipping. Instead, flip food only once or as needed. Over-flipping can disrupt the searing process and prevent grill marks from forming.

3. Wait for Release: When you try to flip food and it sticks to the grates, it's not ready to turn. Wait a bit longer, and it should release easily when it's properly seared.

4. Use a Gentle Touch: When flipping delicate items like fish or vegetables, use a gentle touch to avoid breaking them apart. A grill basket or grilling mat can be helpful for such items.

5. Avoid Squishing: Resist the urge to press down on meats with a spatula. This can cause juices to escape, resulting in dry meat.

6. Safety First: When flipping larger cuts or whole poultry, use grill mitts or gloves to protect your hands from the heat.

Flipping Guidelines for Common Foods

Different foods require specific flipping techniques:

- Burgers: Flip burgers once, about halfway through the recommended cooking time. For medium-rare burgers, aim for an internal temperature of 130-135°F (54-57°C).

- Steaks: For a perfect medium-rare steak, flip once when the meat releases easily from the grill grates. Use a meat thermometer to achieve an internal temperature of 130- 135°F (54-57°C).

- Chicken: Grill chicken pieces skin-side down first to crisp the skin. Flip as needed, and ensure the internal temperature reaches 165°F (74°C).

- Fish: Delicate fish fillets should be flipped gently once during cooking. Cook until the fish flakes easily with a fork and reaches the desired internal temperature.

- Vegetables: Flip vegetables as they become tender and grill marks form. Cooking times may vary depending on the type of vegetable and the thickness of the slices.

By mastering the timing and flipping techniques for grilling, you'll have greater control over the cooking process and consistently achieve delicious, well-cooked dishes. Whether you're grilling steaks, burgers, chicken, fish, or vegetables, these techniques will help you serve up mouthwatering meals that will delight your family and guests.

Smoking Techniques

Types of Wood and Flavors

The choice of wood used for smoking is a crucial element in achieving the desired flavor profile for your smoked dishes. Different types of wood impart unique flavors and aromas to your food, making it an integral part of the smoking process. In this section, we'll explore the various types of wood commonly used for smoking and the flavors they bring to your culinary creations.

Types of Wood for Smoking

1. Hickory:

- Flavor Profile: Hickory is known for its strong, robust, and slightly sweet flavor. It's one of the most popular woods for smoking, especially for pork and beef.
- Best Matches: Pork ribs, pork shoulder (butt), beef brisket, and poultry.

2. Mesquite:

- Flavor Profile: Mesquite wood imparts an intense, earthy, and slightly spicy flavor. It's commonly used in south-western and Tex-Mex cuisine.
- Best Matches: Beef, particularly steaks and burgers, as well as poultry and game meats.

3. Oak:

- Flavor Profile: Oak offers a mild, well-rounded flavor that enhances the natural taste of the meat without overpowering it. It's a versatile wood for smoking.
- Best Matches: Beef, pork, poultry, fish, and even vegeta- bles.

4. Cherry:

- Flavor Profile: Cherry wood provides a mild, fruity, and slightly sweet flavor with a subtle reddish hue. It's a versatile wood for adding a touch of sweetness.
- Best Matches: Pork, poultry, fish, and fruits.

5. Apple:

- Flavor Profile: Applewood is mild, fruity, and sweet, making it a favorite for imparting a delicate smoky flavor without overwhelming the food.
- Best Matches: Pork, poultry, fish, and desserts like smoked apple pie.

6. Pecan:

- Flavor Profile: Pecan wood offers a sweet, nutty flavor with a mild smokiness. It's similar to hickory but milder.
- Best Matches: Pork, poultry, beef, and game meats.

7. Maple:

- Flavor Profile: Maplewood has a mild, sweet, and slightly smoky flavor. It's versatile and complements a variety of dishes.
- Best Matches: Pork, poultry, ham, and vegetables.

8. Alder:

- Flavor Profile: Alderwood is mild, sweet, and delicate, often used for imparting a subtle smoky flavor to fish and seafood.
- Best Matches: Salmon, trout, and other fish, as well as poultry.

Wood Pairing Tips

- Matching Wood to Meat: Consider the intensity of the wood's flavor when pairing it with specific meats. Strong woods like hickory or mesquite work well with bold- flavored meats like beef, while milder woods like apple or cherry are better suited for poultry and fish.
- Experimentation: Don't be afraid to experiment with different wood combinations to discover unique flavor profiles. Mixing woods, such as using a base of oak with a hint of fruitwood, can create exciting results.
- Preparation: When using wood for smoking, it's essential to prepare it correctly. Soak wood chips or chunks in water for about 30 minutes before placing them on the coals or in a smoker box to produce flavorful smoke.
- Moderation: Use wood sparingly, as too much smoke can result in an overpowering, bitter taste. Start with a small amount and adjust based on your taste preferences.

Understanding the characteristics of different types of wood and their flavors allows you to elevate your smoking tech- niques and create a wide range of delicious smoked dishes. Experimentation and careful wood selection will help you achieve the perfect balance of smoky goodness in your culi- nary creations.

Low and Slow Cooking

Low and slow cooking is a fundamental technique in the world of smoking. It involves cooking meats, poultry, or other dishes at low temperatures over an extended period. This method allows the food to absorb smoky flavors while becoming tender and moist. In this section, we'll explore the principles and steps involved in low and slow smoking for exceptional results.

The Benefits of Low and Slow Cooking

1. Tenderization: Slow cooking at lower temperatures breaks down collagen and connective tissues in meat, resulting in tender and juicy results. Tough cuts of meat become melt-in-your-mouth tender.

2. Flavor Infusion: Low and slow cooking allows ample time for smoke to permeate the food, imparting a rich, smoky flavor that complements the natural taste of the ingredients.

3. Moisture Retention: The extended cooking time helps retain moisture, preventing meats from drying out. This results in succulent, flavorful dishes.

Steps for Low and Slow Cooking

1. Select the Right Meat:

   - Choose Tough Cuts: Low and slow cooking is ideal for tougher cuts of meat like pork shoulder, beef brisket, ribs, and whole poultry. These cuts benefit from the extended cooking time.

2. Preparing the Meat:

   - Trim Excess Fat: Trim excess fat to ensure the smoke and seasonings penetrate the meat.
   - Seasoning: Season the meat with a dry rub or marinade, allowing it to rest for several hours or overnight to absorb flavors.
   - Brining (Optional): For poultry or lean meats, consider brining to add moisture and flavor.

3. Preheat the Smoker:

   - Preheat to the Desired Temperature: Preheat your smoker to the target cooking temperature. Low and slow cooking typically ranges from 225°F (107°C) to 275°F (135°C). The exact temperature depends on the recipe and the meat being cooked.

4. Add Smoke:

   - Use Wood Chips or Chunks: Soak wood chips or chunks in water for about 30 minutes. Place them on the hot coals or in a smoker box for continuous smoke production.

5. Place the Meat:

   · Position the Meat: Place the seasoned meat in the smoker. If cooking multiple cuts, ensure there is enough space for smoke and heat circulation.
   · Meat Side Up: Position the meat with the fat side up to allow the melting fat to baste the meat as it cooks.

6. Maintain Consistent Temperature:

   · Monitor Temperature: Use a reliable thermometer to monitor the smoker's temperature. Adjust airflow, vents, or burner settings as needed to maintain a consistent cooking temperature.

7. Patience Is Key:

   · Allow for Adequate Cooking Time: Low and slow cooking is not a rushed process. Be patient and allow the meat to cook slowly, absorbing smoke and developing flavor over several hours.

8. Use a Water Pan (Optional):

   · Water Pan: Some smokers include a water pan to main- tain humidity and prevent excessive drying. Consider using one if your smoker has this feature.

9. Check Doneness:

   · Use a Meat Thermometer: Check the internal tempera- ture of the meat using a meat thermometer. The target temperature varies by the type of meat, but it's typically around 190°F (88°C) for pork and 203°F (95°C) for beef brisket.

10. Rest and Serve:

   · Rest the Meat: After cooking, allow the meat to rest for at least 15-30 minutes. This helps redistribute juices and ensures a juicy final product.
   · Slice and Serve: Slice or shred the meat as desired and serve with your favorite barbecue sauce or side dishes.

Low and slow cooking is a time-honored technique that produces mouthwatering, tender, and smoky results. With patience and attention to detail, you can master this method and create unforgettable smoked dishes that will be the highlight of any barbecue gathering.

Smoking Various Meats and Foods

Smoking is a versatile cooking method that can be used to impart smoky flavor to a wide range of meats, poultry, seafood, and even vegetables and fruits. Each type of food requires specific techniques and considerations to achieve the best results. In this section, we'll explore the smoking techniques for various meats and foods to help you master the art of smoking.

Smoking Meats

1. Pork

Pork Shoulder (Butt):
- Preparation: Trim excess fat and apply a flavorful dry rub or marinade. Allow it to marinate for several hours or overnight.
- Smoking Time: Smoke at 225°F (107°C) until the internal temperature reaches 195-205°F (90-96°C). This may take 1.5 to 2 hours per pound.
- Wood: Hickory or applewood complements pork shoul- der's rich flavor.

Ribs (Baby Back or Spare):
- Preparation: Remove the membrane from the back of the ribs and apply a dry rub or marinade.
- Smoking Time: Smoke at 225°F (107°C) for 3-4 hours for baby back ribs or 5-6 hours for spare ribs.
- Wood: Apple or cherry wood enhances the sweet and savory flavors of ribs.

Pork Loin:
- Preparation: Season with a dry rub or marinade, and op- tionally wrap it with bacon for added flavor and moisture.
- Smoking Time: Smoke at 225°F (107°C) until the internal temperature reaches 145-150°F (63-66°C).
- Wood: Applewood or oak complements the mild flavor of pork loin.

2. Beef

Brisket:
- Preparation: Trim excess fat and apply a generous dry rub.
- Smoking Time: Smoke at 225°F (107°C) for 1.5-2 hours per pound until the internal temperature reaches 195-203°F (90-95°C).
- Wood: Hickory or oak is often used to enhance the rich flavor of brisket.

Steaks and Burgers:
- Preparation: Season with a dry rub or marinade, and let it sit for at least 30 minutes before smoking.
- Smoking Time: Smoke at 225-250°F (107-121°C) for about 1-1.5 hours for steaks or less for burgers, depending on desired doneness.
- Wood: Mesquite or hickory adds a bold flavor to steaks and burgers.

3. Poultry

Chicken (Whole or Parts):

- Preparation: Season with a dry rub or marinade. Brining is optional but can add moisture and flavor.
- Smoking Time: Smoke at 275-325°F (135-163°C) until the internal temperature reaches 165°F (74°C) for chicken parts and 175°F (80°C) for a whole chicken.
- Wood: Apple, cherry, or hickory complement the mild flavor of chicken.

Turkey (Whole or Parts):

- Preparation: Season with a dry rub or brine the turkey for several hours or overnight.
- Smoking Time: Smoke at 225-250°F (107-121°C) until the internal temperature reaches 165°F (74°C) for parts or 175°F (80°C) for a whole turkey.
- Wood: Pecan, apple, or cherry wood provides a sweet and nutty flavor to turkey.

4. Smoking Seafood

Salmon and Trout

- Preparation: Season with a dry rub or marinate with a flavorful mixture.
- Smoking Time: Smoke at 180-200°F (82-93°C) for 1-2 hours or until the fish flakes easily with a fork.
- Wood: Alder or fruitwoods like apple and cherry work well with salmon and trout.

Shrimp and Shellfish

- Preparation: Toss shrimp or shellfish in a seasoned butter or marinade.
- Smoking Time: Smoke at 225-250°F (107-121°C) for about 15-20 minutes until they turn pink and opaque.
- Wood: Mesquite or hickory can add a robust flavor to seafood.

5. Smoking Vegetables and Fruits

Vegetables

- Preparation: Toss vegetables like bell peppers, zucchini, or eggplant in olive oil and seasonings.
- Smoking Time: Smoke at 225-250°F (107-121°C) for 30 minutes to 1 hour, depending on the vegetable's size and desired tenderness.
- Wood: Use mild fruitwoods like apple or cherry for a subtle smoky flavor.

Fruits

- Preparation: Halve or slice fruits like peaches, apples, or pineapple. Optionally, brush with honey or sugar.
- Smoking Time: Smoke at 225-250°F (107-121°C) for 30 minutes to 1 hour, until the fruits are soft and caramelized.
- Wood: Fruitwoods like apple or cherry enhance the natural sweetness of the fruits.

Smoking various meats, seafood, vegetables, and fruits opens up a world of culinary possibilities. By understanding the specific techniques and considerations for each type of food, you can create a diverse range of smoky, flavorful dishes that will impress your family and guests at your next barbecue or smoking session.

Sides and Salads

Grilled Corn on the Cob with Parmesan Butter

Prep Time: 10 min | Grilling Time: 15 min | Total Time: 25 min
Servings: 4

Ingredients:
For the Grilled Corn:

- 4 ears of fresh corn on the cob, husks removed
- Olive oil (for brushing)
- Salt and black pepper, to taste

For the Parmesan Butter:

- 1/2 cup unsalted butter, softened
- 1/2 cup grated Parmesan cheese
- 2 cloves garlic, minced
- 2 tablespoons fresh parsley, finely chopped
- 1 tablespoon fresh chives, finely chopped (optional)
- Salt and black pepper, to taste

Instructions:

1. Prepare the Parmesan Butter:

- In a mixing bowl, combine the softened butter, grated Parmesan cheese, minced garlic, fresh parsley, and chopped chives (if using).
- Season the mixture with salt and black pepper to taste.
- Use a fork or a spatula to thoroughly blend all the ingre- dients together. Once well combined, set the Parmesan butter aside.

2. Preheat the Grill:

- Preheat your grill to medium-high heat (about 350-400°F or 175-200°C).

3. Grill the Corn:

- Brush each ear of corn with a light coating of olive oil and season with salt and black pepper.
- Place the corn directly on the grill grates.
- Grill the corn for about 10-15 minutes, turning occasion- ally until it's charred and tender. The cooking time may vary depending on the heat of your grill and the size of the corn.

4. Coat with Parmesan Butter:

- When the corn is done, remove it from the grill.
- While the corn is still hot, generously slather each ear with the prepared Parmesan butter. The heat from the corn will help melt and spread the butter.

5. Serve:

- Serve your grilled corn on the cob with Parmesan butter immediately while it's hot and the butter is melting.
- Optionally, garnish with additional grated Parmesan cheese, chopped fresh herbs, or a sprinkle of red pepper flakes for extra flavor.

6. Enjoy:

- Enjoy your grilled corn on the cob with Parmesan butter as a delicious side dish for your next barbecue or summer meal!

Grilling corn on the cob and topping it with savory Parmesan butter creates a mouthwatering combination of sweet and savory flavors. It's a perfect addition to any outdoor gathering or summer cookout.

Smoked Mac and Cheese

Preparation Time: 20 min | Smoking Time: 1 hour

Servings: 6-8

Ingredients:

- 16 ounces (1 pound) elbow macaroni or your favorite pasta
- 4 cups shredded sharp cheddar cheese
- 1 cup shredded mozzarella cheese
- 2 cups milk (whole or 2% recommended)
- 1/4 cup unsalted butter
- 1/4 cup all-purpose flour
- 1 teaspoon salt, or to taste
- 1/2 teaspoon black pepper, or to taste
- 1/2 teaspoon paprika
- 1/4 teaspoon cayenne pepper (optional, for a little heat)
- Cooking spray or butter (for greasing the dish)

For Smoking:

- Your choice of smoking wood chips (hickory, mesquite, or applewood recommended)

Equipment:

- Smoker
- Aluminum foil or a disposable aluminum pan

Instructions:

Cooking the Pasta:

1. Cook the Pasta: Follow the package instructions to cook the elbow macaroni or pasta until it's al dente. Drain and set it aside.

Preparing the Cheese Sauce:

1. Make the Roux: In a large saucepan on the grill, melt the unsalted butter over medium heat. Add the all-purpose flour and stir continuously for about 1-2 minutes until the mixture turns a light golden color. This is your roux.

2. Add Milk: Gradually pour in the milk while continuing to whisk the roux to avoid lumps. Cook for a few minutes until the mixture thickens and becomes smooth.

3. Season the Sauce: Add the salt, black pepper, paprika, and cayenne pepper (if using). Stir to combine.

4. Add Cheese: Reduce the heat to low, and gradually add the shredded sharp cheddar cheese and shredded mozzarella cheese. Stir until the cheese is fully melted, and the sauce is creamy and smooth. Taste and adjust the seasoning if needed.

Smoking the Mac and Cheese:

1. Preheat the Smoker: Preheat your smoker to 225°F (107°C) using your choice of smoking wood chips. Hick- ory, mesquite, or applewood chips work well for a smoky flavor.

2. Grease the Dish: Grease a disposable aluminum pan or a heatproof dish with cooking spray or butter to prevent sticking.

3. Combine Pasta and Cheese Sauce: In a large mixing bowl, combine the cooked pasta and the prepared cheese sauce. Stir until the pasta is evenly coated with the creamy cheese mixture.

4. Transfer to the Dish: Transfer the mac and cheese mixture to the greased dish or pan, spreading it out evenly.

5. Smoke the Mac and Cheese: Place the dish in the preheated smoker. Close the smoker's lid and smoke the mac and cheese for about 1 hour, or until it absorbs a delicious smoky flavor and develops a golden crust on top.

Serving:

1. Serve Hot: Remove the smoked mac and cheese from the smoker and let it cool for a few minutes before serving. Scoop out generous portions and enjoy your creamy and smoky mac and cheese!

Smoked Mac and Cheese is a delightful twist on the classic comfort food, perfect for barbecue gatherings or as a side dish for any smoked meats. The smokiness adds a unique and savory dimension to the creamy cheese sauce, making it a crowd-pleaser for all ages.

Smoked Baked Potato

Preparation Time: 10 min | Smoking Time: 2-3 hours | Total Time: 2 hours 10 min - 3 hours 10 min
Servings: 4

Ingredients:

- 4 large russet potatoes
- Olive oil
- Salt
- Black pepper
- Toppings of your choice (butter, sour cream, shredded cheese, chives, bacon bits, etc.)

Equipment:

- Smoker
- Aluminum foil

Instructions:

1. Preheat the Smoker:

- Preheat your smoker to 225°F (107°C) using your choice of smoking wood chips (hickory, apple, or any flavor you prefer) according to the manufacturer's instructions.

2. Prepare the Potatoes:

- Wash and scrub the potatoes thoroughly to remove any dirt. Pat them dry with paper towels.
- Prick each potato several times with a fork to allow steam to escape during smoking.

3. Season the Potatoes:

- Rub each potato with a light coating of olive oil to help the skin become crispy during smoking.
- Season the potatoes generously with salt and black pep- per.

4. Smoke the Potatoes:

- Place the seasoned potatoes directly on the smoker grates.
- Close the smoker lid and smoke the potatoes at 225°F (107°C) for 2-3 hours, or until the potatoes are tender and easily pierced with a fork.

5. Check for Doneness:

- About halfway through the smoking time, you can check the potatoes for doneness by inserting a fork or skewer into the center. If it goes in with little resistance, they are done.

6. Serve:

- Once the potatoes are done, remove them from the smoker.
- Carefully slice each potato open lengthwise, creating a pocket for your toppings.

7. Add Toppings:

- Add your favorite baked potato toppings, such as butter, sour cream, shredded cheese, chives, bacon bits, or any other toppings you prefer.

8. Enjoy:

- Serve your smoked baked potatoes hot as a delicious and smoky side dish.

These smoked baked potatoes have a rich, smoky flavor and a crispy skin, making them a fantastic accompaniment to grilled or smoked meats. Customize them with your favorite toppings for a perfect outdoor meal.

Smoked Baby Potato Salad with Mustard Dressing

Prep Time: 15 min | Smoking Time: 1-1.5 hours | Total Time: 1 hour 15 min - 1 hour 45 min
Servings: 6

Ingredients:
For the Smoked Baby Potatoes:

· 2 pounds baby potatoes, preferably red or Yukon Gold
· Olive oil
· Salt and black pepper, to taste
· 1 teaspoon paprika
· 1 teaspoon garlic powder
· 1 teaspoon onion powder
· Smoking wood chips (hickory, apple, or your choice)

For the Mustard Dressing:

· 1/2 cup mayonnaise
· 2 tablespoons Dijon mustard
· 1 tablespoon whole-grain mustard
· 2 tablespoons apple cider vinegar
· 1 tablespoon honey
· 1 clove garlic, minced
· Salt and black pepper, to taste

For the Salad:

· 4 hard-boiled eggs, chopped
· 4 green onions, thinly sliced
· 2 celery stalks, finely chopped
· 2 tablespoons fresh dill, chopped (optional)
· 2 tablespoons fresh parsley, chopped (optional)
· Pickles, chopped (optional)

Instructions:

1. Preheat the Smoker:

· Preheat your smoker to 225°F (107°C) using your choice of smoking wood chips (hickory, apple, or any flavor you prefer) according to the manufacturer's instructions.

2. Prepare the Baby Potatoes:

- Wash and scrub the baby potatoes thoroughly. Pat them dry with paper towels.

3. Season the Baby Potatoes:

- In a large bowl, toss the baby potatoes with olive oil, salt, black pepper, paprika, garlic powder, and onion powder. Ensure they are well coated.

4. Smoke the Baby Potatoes:

- Place the seasoned baby potatoes directly on the smoker grates.
- Close the smoker lid and smoke the baby potatoes at 225°F (107°C) for 1-1.5 hours, or until they are tender and have a light smoky flavor. Stir the potatoes occasionally for even smoking.

5. Make the Mustard Dressing:

- In a small bowl, whisk together the mayonnaise, Di- jon mustard, whole-grain mustard, apple cider vinegar, honey, minced garlic, salt, and black pepper. Adjust the seasoning to your taste.

6. Assemble the Salad:

- In a large mixing bowl, combine the smoked baby pota- toes, chopped hard-boiled eggs, sliced green onions, cho- pped celery, fresh dill (if using), and fresh parsley (if using).
- Optionally, add chopped pickles for extra flavor.

7. Dress the Salad:

- Pour the mustard dressing over the baby potato salad mixture.
- Gently toss everything together until the salad is well coated with the dressing.

8. Chill and Serve:

- Cover the salad and refrigerate for at least 1 hour to allow the flavors to meld.
- Serve your smoked baby potato salad with mustard dress- ing cold as a delicious and smoky side dish for picnics, barbecues, or any outdoor gathering.

This smoked baby potato salad with mustard dressing offers the smoky depth of flavor you love, combined with the ten- derness of baby potatoes. It's a delightful addition to your outdoor meals and gatherings.

Smoked Garlic Mashed Potatoes

Prep Time: 15 min | Smoking Time: 1.5-2 hours | Total Time: 1 hour 45 min - 2 hours 15 min
Servings: 6-8

Ingredients:

For Smoking the Potatoes:

- 4 pounds Russet or Yukon Gold potatoes, peeled and cut into chunks
- 4-6 cloves garlic, unpeeled
- Olive oil
- Salt and black pepper, to taste
- Smoking wood chips (hickory, apple, or your choice)

For Making the Mashed Potatoes:

- 1 cup heavy cream or milk (adjust to your preferred creaminess)
- 1/2 cup unsalted butter (1 stick)
- Salt and black pepper, to taste
- Fresh chives or parsley, chopped, for garnish (optional)

Instructions:

1. Preheat the Smoker:

- Preheat your smoker to 225°F (107°C) using your choice of smoking wood chips (hickory, apple, or any flavor you prefer) according to the manufacturer's instructions.

2. Prepare the Potatoes and Garlic:

- Peel and cut the potatoes into chunks of roughly equal size.
- Place the unpeeled garlic cloves on a piece of aluminum foil, drizzle with olive oil, and wrap them up in the foil to create a garlic packet.

3. Smoke the Potatoes and Garlic:

- Place the potato chunks and the garlic packet directly on the smoker grates.
- Close the smoker lid and smoke the potatoes and garlic at 225°F (107°C) for 1.5-2 hours or until the potatoes are tender and have absorbed a subtle smoky flavor. Stir the potatoes occasionally for even smoking.

4. Make the Mashed Potatoes:

- Remove the smoked potatoes and garlic from the smoker.
- Squeeze the roasted garlic cloves out of their skins into a large mixing bowl.
- Mash the smoked potatoes and roasted garlic together until well combined.
- In a saucepan, heat the heavy cream or milk and butter over low heat until the butter is melted. Do not boil.
- Pour the warm cream-butter mixture over the mashed potatoes and continue to mash until you reach your desired level of creaminess.
- Season the smoked garlic mashed potatoes with salt and black pepper to taste.

5. Serve:

- Transfer the smoked garlic mashed potatoes to a serving dish.
- Garnish with fresh chives or parsley if desired.

6. Enjoy:

- Serve your smoked garlic mashed potatoes hot as a fla- vorful and smoky side dish that complements a variety of main courses, especially grilled or smoked meats.

These smoked garlic mashed potatoes are a delightful twist on a classic favorite, adding a subtle smoky depth of flavor. They're perfect for enhancing your outdoor meals and gath- erings.

Grilled Sweet Potato Wedges

Prep Time: 15 min | Grilling Time: 20-25 min | Total Time: 35-40 min
Servings: 4

Ingredients:

- 2 large sweet potatoes
- 2 tablespoons olive oil
- 1 teaspoon smoked paprika
- 1/2 teaspoon garlic powder
- 1/2 teaspoon onion powder
- 1/2 teaspoon chili powder (adjust to taste)
- Salt and black pepper, to taste
- Fresh parsley or cilantro for garnish (optional)

Instructions:

1. Preheat the Grill:

- Preheat your grill to medium-high heat (about 350-400°F or 175-200°C).

2. Prepare the Sweet Potatoes:

- Wash and scrub the sweet potatoes thoroughly. Pat them dry with a paper towel.
- Cut the sweet potatoes into wedges. You can do this by cutting each sweet potato in half lengthwise, and then cutting each half into wedges.

3. Season the Sweet Potato Wedges:

- In a large mixing bowl, combine the sweet potato wedges, olive oil, smoked paprika, garlic powder, onion powder, chili powder, salt, and black pepper.
- Toss the sweet potato wedges until they are evenly coated with the seasoning mixture.

4. Grill the Sweet Potato Wedges:

- Place the seasoned sweet potato wedges directly on the grill grates.
- Grill for about 20-25 minutes, turning occasionally, or until the sweet potatoes are tender and have grill marks. Cooking time may vary depending on the thickness of your wedges and the heat of your grill.

5. Serve:

- Remove the grilled sweet potato wedges from the grill and place them on a serving platter.
- Garnish with fresh parsley or cilantro if desired.

6. Enjoy:

- Serve your grilled sweet potato wedges hot as a delicious and healthy side dish or snack.

These grilled sweet potato wedges are a tasty and nutritious option for your next barbecue or outdoor gathering. The smoky flavor and seasoning make them a perfect accompani- ment to grilled meats or as a standalone appetizer.

Smoked Garlic Bulbs

Preparation Time: 10 min | Smoking Time: 1-2 hours
Servings: Varies

Ingredients:

- Whole bulbs of garlic
- Olive oil
- Salt and black pepper to taste

Equipment:

- Smoker
- Smoking wood chips (such as hickory or applewood)

Instructions:

Preparing the Garlic Bulbs:

1. Select the Garlic Bulbs: Choose as many whole bulbs of garlic as you desire. Garlic becomes sweet and mellow when smoked, making it a versatile ingredient.
2. Trim the Tops: Trim about 1/4 inch from the top of each garlic bulb to expose the cloves. This will help the smoke penetrate the garlic.
3. Peel Loose Outer Layers: Gently remove any loose, papery outer layers from the garlic bulbs, but leave the bulbs intact.

Preparing the Smoker:

1. Preheat the Smoker: Preheat your smoker to a tempera-ture of 225-250°F (107-121°C). For this recipe, you can use a mild smoking wood like applewood, hickory, or cherry.
2. Soak the Wood Chips: While the smoker is preheating, soak the smoking wood chips in water for about 30 minutes. Drain them before using.

Smoking the Garlic Bulbs:

1. Drizzle with Olive Oil: Place the prepared garlic bulbs on a piece of aluminum foil. Drizzle a small amount of olive oil over the exposed cloves. Season with a pinch of salt and black pepper to taste.
2. Wrap in Foil: Wrap the garlic bulbs tightly in the aluminum foil, creating a sealed pouch. This will help infuse the garlic with smoky flavor as it smokes.

3. Add the Wood Chips: Once the smoker is at the desired temperature, add the soaked wood chips to the smoker's wood chip tray or use a smoking tube to generate smoke.

4. Smoke the Garlic Bulbs: Place the foil-wrapped garlic pouch directly on the smoker grates. Close the smoker's lid and smoke the garlic bulbs at the preheated tempera- ture for 1-2 hours. The longer you smoke them, the more intense the smoky flavor will be. Garlic is ready when it becomes soft and develops a lovely smoky aroma.

Resting and Serving:

1. Cool and Unwrap: Carefully remove the smoked garlic bulbs from the smoker and allow them to cool slightly. Once they are cool enough to handle, carefully unwrap them from the foil pouch.

2. Extract the Garlic: Squeeze or gently press the roasted garlic cloves out of their skins. The garlic will be soft, fragrant, and easily spreadable.

3. Serve: Your Smoked Garlic Bulbs are now ready to be served. Use the smoked garlic as a spread on bread, mix it into mashed potatoes, blend it into sauces, or add it to your favorite recipes for a rich and smoky garlic flavor.

Smoked Garlic Bulbs add depth and complexity to your dishes with their smoky, sweet, and aromatic qualities. Enjoy the unique flavor that smoking brings to this versatile kitchen staple.

Balsamic Grilled Vegetables

Preparation Time: 15 min | Marinating Time: 30 min | Cooking Time: 10-12 min
Servings: 4

Ingredients:
For the Balsamic Marinade:

- 1/4 cup balsamic vinegar
- 3 tablespoons olive oil
- 2 cloves garlic, minced
- 1 teaspoon Dijon mustard
- 1 teaspoon honey (optional for added sweetness)
- 1/2 teaspoon dried oregano
- Salt and freshly ground black pepper, to taste For the Grilled Vegetables:
- 2 bell peppers (any color), seeded and cut into strips
- 2 zucchini, sliced diagonally
- 1 bunch asparagus, trimmed
- 1 red onion, cut into wedges
- 8-10 cherry tomatoes (optional)
- Wooden skewers (soaked in water for 30 minutes to prevent burning)
- Fresh basil leaves (for garnish, optional)

Instructions:
Preparing the Balsamic Marinade:

1. Create the Balsamic Marinade:

- In a bowl, combine the balsamic vinegar, olive oil, minced garlic, Dijon mustard, honey (if using), dried oregano, salt, and freshly ground black pepper.
- Whisk the ingredients together to create a flavorful bal- samic marinade.

Marinating and Grilling the Vegetables:

2. Marinate the Vegetables:

- Place the prepared bell pepper strips, zucchini slices, asparagus, red onion wedges, and cherry tomatoes (if using) in a large resealable plastic bag or a shallow dish.

3. Pour in the Marinade:

- Pour the balsamic marinade over the vegetables.

4. Seal and Marinate:

- Seal the bag (or cover the dish) and refrigerate for at least 30 minutes, allowing the vegetables to absorb the balsamic flavors.

5. Preheat the Grill:

- Preheat your grill to medium-high heat, around 375- 400°F (190-204°C) for direct grilling.

6. Thread the Skewers:

- · Thread the marinated vegetables onto the wooden skew- ers, alternating the types of vegetables for a colorful mix.

7. Brush with Marinade:

- · Brush the skewered vegetables with the remaining bal- samic marinade to enhance the flavor.

8. Grill for 4-5 Minutes per Side:

- · Place the vegetable skewers on the preheated grill grates.

- Grill for about 4-5 minutes per side, or until the veg- etables are tender and have grill marks. The cherry tomatoes may become slightly charred.

Serving Balsamic Grilled Vegetables:

1. Plate the Vegetables:

- Transfer the grilled vegetable skewers to a serving platter.

2. Garnish and Serve:

- Garnish with fresh basil leaves, if desired.

Enjoy your Balsamic Grilled Vegetables, featuring a medley of bell peppers, zucchini, asparagus, and red onions, all marinated in balsamic goodness and grilled to perfection. It's a fantastic side dish that pairs well with various main courses.

Grilled Vegetable Platter

Preparation Time: 15 min | Grilling Time: 15-20 min
Servings: 4

Ingredients:

- 2 bell peppers (any color), cut into thick strips
- 2 medium zucchini, sliced diagonally into 1/2-inch thick pieces
- 1 bunch of asparagus, tough ends trimmed
- 2-3 tablespoons olive oil
- Salt and black pepper to taste
- 2 cloves garlic, minced (optional, for extra flavor)
- 1 teaspoon dried Italian seasoning (or a blend of dried herbs like oregano, thyme, and rosemary)
- Juice of 1 lemon (for drizzling, optional)
- Fresh parsley or basil leaves, for garnish (optional)

Instructions:

1. Preheat the Grill: Preheat your grill to medium-high heat (about 400-450°F or 200-230°C).

2. Prepare the Vegetables: In a large mixing bowl, combine the bell pepper strips, zucchini slices, and trimmed asparagus. If using minced garlic, sprinkle it over the vegetables.

3. Season and Oil: Drizzle the olive oil over the vegetables and season with salt, black pepper, and the dried Italian seasoning. Toss the vegetables until they are evenly coated with the oil and seasonings.

4. Grill the Vegetables: Place the vegetables directly on the grill grates or use a grill basket to prevent them from falling through. Grill for about 15-20 minutes, turning them occasionally, until they are tender and have grill marks. The exact grilling time may vary depending on your grill's heat.

5. Serve: Once the vegetables are grilled to your desired level of tenderness and have beautiful grill marks, re-move them from the grill. Optionally, drizzle them with fresh lemon juice for a zesty touch. Garnish with fresh parsley or basil leaves.

6. Enjoy: Serve your Grilled Vegetable Platter as a colorful and flavorful side dish. It pairs wonderfully with grilled meats, fish, or as part of a vegetarian meal. The vibrant colors and smoky flavor will make this dish a hit at any gathering.

Feel free to customize this recipe by adding your favorite vegetables or experimenting with different seasonings. Enjoy your grilled vegetable platter as a healthy and delicious addition to your next outdoor meal!

Spicy Grilled Cauliflower Steaks

Preparation Time: 15 min | Marinating Time: 30 min | Cooking Time: 15-20 min
Servings: 4

Ingredients:
For the Spicy Rub:

- 2 teaspoons smoked paprika
- 1 teaspoon ground cumin
- 1 teaspoon chili powder
- 1/2 teaspoon cayenne pepper (adjust to your preferred level of spiciness)
- 1/2 teaspoon garlic powder
- 1/2 teaspoon onion powder
- 1/2 teaspoon salt
- 1/4 teaspoon freshly ground black pepper
- 2 tablespoons olive oil For the Cauliflower Steaks:
- 1 large head of cauliflower
- Olive oil for brushing
- Fresh cilantro leaves (for garnish, optional)
- Lime wedges (for garnish, optional)

Instructions:
Preparing the Spicy Rub:

1. Create the Spicy Rub:

- In a small bowl, combine the smoked paprika, ground cumin, chili powder, cayenne pepper, garlic powder, onion powder, salt, freshly ground black pepper, and olive oil.
- Mix the ingredients thoroughly to create a spicy rub.

Preparing and Grilling the Cauliflower Steaks:

1. Preheat the Grill:

- Preheat your grill to medium-high heat, around 375- 400°F (190-204°C) for direct grilling.

2. Prepare the Cauliflower:

- Remove the leaves and trim the stem of the cauliflower head.
- Cut the cauliflower into 1-inch thick slices to create "steaks." Be careful to keep them intact.

3. Brush with Olive Oil:

- Brush both sides of the cauliflower steaks lightly with olive oil.

4. Season with Spicy Rub:

- Generously sprinkle the spicy rub mixture over both sides of the cauliflower steaks, pressing it onto the surface to adhere.

5. Marinate for 30 Minutes:

- Place the seasoned cauliflower steaks on a plate and let them marinate for about 30 minutes at room temperature. This allows the flavors to infuse.

6. Grill the Cauliflower Steaks:

- Place the cauliflower steaks on the preheated grill grates.

7. Grill for 7-10 Minutes per Side:

- Grill the cauliflower steaks for about 7-10 minutes per side, or until they are tender and have grill marks. Cook- ing time may vary depending on the thickness of the steaks.

Serving Spicy Grilled Cauliflower Steaks:

1. Remove from Grill:

- Carefully remove the grilled cauliflower steaks from the grill.

2. Garnish and Serve:

- Garnish with fresh cilantro leaves and lime wedges, if desired.

Enjoy your Spicy Grilled Cauliflower Steaks as a flavorful and spicy side dish or even as a vegetarian main course. The smoky and spicy rub enhances the natural flavors of the cauliflower, making it a delicious and satisfying option for your grill.

Sesame Grilled Eggplant

Preparation Time: 15 min | Marinating Time: 30 min | Cooking Time: 10-12 min
Servings: 4

Ingredients:
For the Marinade:

- · 1/4 cup soy sauce
- · 2 tablespoons sesame oil
- · 2 tablespoons rice vinegar
- · 2 cloves garlic, minced
- · 1 tablespoon honey or brown sugar
- · 1/2 teaspoon red pepper flakes (adjust to your preferred level of spiciness)
- · 1 tablespoon toasted sesame seeds
- · Salt and freshly ground black pepper, to taste For the Grilled Eggplant:
- · 2 medium-sized eggplants
- · Olive oil for brushing
- · Fresh cilantro leaves (for garnish, optional)
- · Lime wedges (for garnish, optional)

Instructions:
Preparing the Marinade:

1. Create the Marinade:

- · In a bowl, combine the soy sauce, sesame oil, rice vinegar, minced garlic, honey or brown sugar, red pepper flakes, toasted sesame seeds, salt, and freshly ground black pepper.
- · Mix the ingredients thoroughly to create a flavorful mari- nade.

Marinating and Grilling the Eggplant:

1. Preheat the Grill:

- Preheat your grill to medium-high heat, around 375- 400°F (190-204°C) for direct grilling.

2. Prepare the Eggplant:

- Cut the eggplants into 1/2-inch thick slices. You can leave the skin on or peel it, depending on your preference.

3. Marinate the Eggplant:

- Place the eggplant slices in a shallow dish.
- Pour the sesame and soy sauce marinade over the egg- plant slices, ensuring they are well coated.
- Use a brush or your hands to evenly distribute the mari- nade.

4. Marinate for 30 Minutes:

- Cover the dish and let the eggplant slices marinate for about 30 minutes at room temperature. This allows the flavors to infuse.

5. Brush with Olive Oil:

- Brush both sides of the marinated eggplant slices lightly with olive oil.

6. Grill the Eggplant:

- Place the eggplant slices on the preheated grill grates.

7. Grill for 5-6 Minutes per Side:

- Grill the eggplant slices for about 5-6 minutes per side, or until they are tender and have grill marks. Cooking time may vary depending on the thickness of the slices.

Serving Sesame Grilled Eggplant:

1. Remove from Grill:

- Carefully remove the grilled eggplant slices from the grill.

2. Garnish and Serve:

- Garnish with fresh cilantro leaves and lime wedges, if desired.

Enjoy your Sesame Grilled Eggplant as a delicious and savory side dish or appetizer. The sesame and soy sauce marinade adds a wonderful depth of flavor to the grilled eggplant, making it a fantastic addition to your outdoor dining experience.

Mesquite Smoked Tomatoes

Preparation Time: 10 min | Smoking Time: 1-2 hours
Servings: Varies

Ingredients:

- Ripe tomatoes (any variety you prefer)
- Olive oil
- Salt and black pepper to taste

Equipment:

- Smoker
- Smoking wood chips (mesquite)

Instructions:

Preparing the Tomatoes:

1. Select the Tomatoes: Choose ripe tomatoes of your preferred variety. Smaller tomatoes like cherry or grape tomatoes work well, but you can also use larger ones. The choice is yours.
2. Wash and Slice: Wash the tomatoes thoroughly and then slice them in half. For larger tomatoes, you can slice them into thick rounds. The goal is to expose the tomato flesh to the smoke.

Preparing the Smoker:

1. Preheat the Smoker: Preheat your smoker to a tempera- ture of 225-250°F (107-121°C). For this recipe, mesquite wood chips are ideal for their strong smoky flavor.
2. Soak the Wood Chips: While the smoker is preheating, soak the mesquite wood chips in water for about 30 minutes. Drain them before using.

Smoking the Tomatoes:

1. Drizzle with Olive Oil: Place the sliced tomatoes on a wire rack or a grill tray suitable for your smoker. Drizzle a small amount of olive oil over the exposed tomato flesh. This will help the smoke adhere to the tomatoes.
2. Season with Salt and Pepper: Season the tomatoes with a pinch of salt and a dash of black pepper to taste.
3. Add the Wood Chips: Once the smoker is at the desired temperature, add the soaked mesquite wood chips to the smoker's wood chip tray or use a smoking tube to generate smoke.
4. Smoke the Tomatoes: Place the rack or tray with the tomatoes on the smoker grates. Close the smoker's lid and smoke

the tomatoes at the preheated temperature for 1-2 hours. The longer you smoke them, the more intense the smoky flavor will be. The tomatoes are ready when they have a slightly wrinkled appearance and have absorbed a delicious smoky aroma.

Resting and Using:

1. Remove and Cool: Carefully remove the smoked toma- toes from the smoker and allow them to cool to room temperature.

2. Serve or Store: You can use Mesquite Smoked Tomatoes in various dishes. They make excellent additions to pasta sauces, salsas, salads, or as toppings for grilled meats and burgers. Store any leftovers in an airtight container in the refrigerator for future use.

Mesquite Smoked Tomatoes add a robust smoky dimension to your favorite dishes, elevating their flavor and making them stand out. Experiment with these smoked tomatoes to discover new and exciting culinary possibilities.

Grilled Tomatoes

Prep Time: 10 min | Grilling Time: 5-7 min | Total Time: 15-17 min
Servings: 4

Ingredients:

- 4 ripe tomatoes (Roma or beefsteak tomatoes work well)
- 2 tablespoons olive oil
- 2 cloves garlic, minced
- 1 teaspoon dried basil (or 2 tablespoons fresh basil, chopped)
- Salt and black pepper, to taste
- Grated Parmesan cheese (optional, for serving)

Instructions:

1. Preheat the Grill:

- Preheat your grill to medium-high heat (about 350-400°F or 175-200°C).

2. Prepare the Tomatoes:

- Wash and dry the tomatoes. Slice them in half hori- zontally, so you have two thick tomato slices from each tomato.

3. Season the Tomatoes:

- In a small bowl, combine the olive oil, minced garlic, dried basil (or fresh basil), salt, and black pepper.
- Brush both sides of the tomato slices with the olive oil mixture.

4. Grill the Tomatoes:

- Place the seasoned tomato slices directly on the grill grates, cut side down.
- Grill for about 2-3 minutes on each side, or until the tomatoes have grill marks and are slightly softened.

5. Serve:

- Remove the grilled tomato slices from the grill and place them on a serving platter.

6. Optional Topping:

· If desired, sprinkle the grilled tomatoes with grated Parmesan cheese while they are still hot.

7. Enjoy:

· Serve your grilled tomatoes as a tasty side dish or appe- tizer. They make a perfect complement to grilled meats, salads, or as a simple and flavorful snack.

Grilled tomatoes are a delightful addition to your outdoor meals. They take just a few minutes to prepare, and the grill adds a smoky flavor that enhances their natural sweetness. Enjoy them with your favorite seasonings and toppings for a delicious treat.

Smoked Cheese-Stuffed Jalapeños

Prep Time: 20 min | Smoking Time: 1 hour | Total Time: 1 hour 20 min
Servings: 6-8 (24 stuffed jalapeños)

Ingredients:

- 12-16 large fresh jalapeño peppers
- 8 ounces cream cheese, softened
- 1 cup shredded cheddar cheese
- 1/2 cup shredded mozzarella cheese
- 2 cloves garlic, minced
- 1 teaspoon onion powder
- 1/2 teaspoon smoked paprika (optional)
- 1/2 teaspoon black pepper
- 1/4 teaspoon salt
- 12-16 slices of bacon, cut in half (1 slice per stuffed jalapeño)
- Toothpicks, for securing the bacon

Instructions:

1. Prepare the Jalapeños:

- Wearing disposable gloves, cut the jalapeño peppers in half lengthwise. Remove the seeds and membranes to reduce their spiciness. Be cautious not to touch your face or eyes while handling the peppers.

2. Make the Cheese Filling:

- In a mixing bowl, combine the softened cream cheese, shredded cheddar cheese, shredded mozzarella cheese, minced garlic, onion powder, smoked paprika (if using), black pepper, and salt. Mix until all the ingredients are well combined.

3. Stuff the Jalapeños:

- Fill each jalapeño half with the cheese mixture, ensuring they are evenly and generously stuffed.

4. Wrap with Bacon:

- Wrap each stuffed jalapeño half with a half-slice of bacon. Secure the bacon with toothpicks, making sure to insert them through the ends of the bacon to hold it in place.

5. Preheat the Smoker:

- Preheat your smoker to 225°F (107°C) using your choice of smoking wood chips (hickory, apple, or any flavor you prefer) according to the manufacturer's instructions.

6. Smoke the Jalapeños:

- Place the bacon-wrapped, cheese-stuffed jalapeños di- rectly on the smoker grates.
- Smoke at 225°F (107°C) for approximately 1 hour, or until the bacon is crispy and the jalapeños are tender.

7. Serve:

- Carefully remove the smoked cheese-stuffed jalapeños from the smoker and let them cool slightly.

8. Enjoy:

- Serve your smoked cheese-stuffed jalapeños as a flavorful and spicy appetizer or snack. Be sure to remove the toothpicks before serving.

These smoked cheese-stuffed jalapeños are a delicious com- bination of spicy, creamy, and smoky flavors. They're perfect for a game day snack or as a crowd-pleasing appetizer at your next gathering. Adjust the number of jalapeños to suit your spice tolerance, and enjoy the deliciousness of these smoky, cheesy bites!

Smoked Stuffed Peppers

Prep Time: 30 min | Smoking Time: 2-2.5 hours | Total Time: 2 hours 30 min - 3 hours
Servings: 6 stuffed peppers

Ingredients:
For the Stuffed Peppers:

- 6 large bell peppers (any color), tops removed and seeds removed
- 1 cup long-grain white rice
- 2 cups water or vegetable broth (for cooking rice)
- 1 pound ground beef or ground turkey (optional)
- 1 small onion, finely chopped
- 2 cloves garlic, minced
- 1 cup diced tomatoes (canned or fresh)
- 1 cup corn kernels (fresh, frozen, or canned)
- 1 cup black beans, drained and rinsed
- 1 cup shredded cheddar cheese
- 1 teaspoon chili powder
- 1/2 teaspoon cumin
- Salt and black pepper, to taste
- Olive oil for brushing

For Smoking:

- Smoking wood chips (hickory, apple, or your choice)

Instructions:

1. Preheat the Smoker:

- Preheat your smoker to 225°F (107°C) using your choice of smoking wood chips (hickory, apple, or any flavor you prefer) according to the manufacturer's instructions.

2. Cook the Rice:

- In a saucepan, bring 2 cups of water or vegetable broth to a boil.
- Add the rice, reduce the heat to low, cover, and simmer for about 15-20 minutes, or until the rice is tender and the liquid is absorbed. Remove from heat and fluff with a fork.

3. Prepare the Filling:

- In a large skillet, heat olive oil over medium heat. If using ground meat, add it and cook until browned. If not using meat, simply heat the olive oil.
- Add the chopped onion and garlic to the skillet and sauté until they become translucent.
- Stir in the diced tomatoes, corn kernels, black beans, chili powder, cumin, salt, and black pepper. Cook for an additional 3-5 minutes, allowing the flavors to meld.
- Add the cooked rice to the skillet and mix everything together. Remove from heat.

4. Stuff the Peppers:

- Stuff each bell pepper with the rice and vegetable mixture, pressing down gently to pack the filling.
- Top each stuffed pepper with shredded cheddar cheese.

5. Smoke the Stuffed Peppers:

- Place the stuffed peppers directly on the smoker grates.
- Close the smoker lid and smoke the peppers at 225°F (107°C) for about 2-2.5 hours, or until the peppers are tender, and the cheese is melted and slightly golden.

6. Serve:

- Carefully remove the smoked stuffed peppers from the smoker and place them on a serving platter.

7. Enjoy:

- Serve your smoked stuffed peppers hot as a flavorful and smoky main dish. These are perfect for a complete meal or as a side dish to complement your barbecue spread.

Smoked stuffed peppers are a delicious twist on a classic dish, adding a smoky depth of flavor to the hearty combination of rice, vegetables, and cheese. They make for an impressive and satisfying meal straight from the smoker.

Grilled Portobello Mushrooms

Preparation Time: 10 min | Marinating Time: 20-30 min | Grilling Time: 8-10 min
Total Time: 40-50 min
Servings: 4

Ingredients:
For the Portobello Marinade:

- 4 large portobello mushroom caps, stems removed
- 1/4 cup balsamic vinegar
- 1/4 cup olive oil
- 2 cloves garlic, minced
- 2 tablespoons fresh parsley, chopped
- 1 teaspoon dried oregano
- Salt and black pepper, to taste

For Serving:

- Buns or lettuce leaves (for serving, optional)
- Toppings of your choice (lettuce, tomato, onion, cheese, etc.)

Instructions:

1. Clean and Prep the Portobello Mushrooms:

- Gently clean the portobello mushroom caps with a damp paper towel to remove any dirt. Remove the stems and use a spoon to scrape out the gills from the underside of the caps.

2. Prepare the Marinade:

- In a bowl, whisk together the balsamic vinegar, olive oil, minced garlic, chopped fresh parsley, dried oregano, salt, and black pepper to create the marinade.

3. Marinate the Mushrooms:

- Place the cleaned portobello mushroom caps in a shallow dish or a resealable plastic bag.
- Pour the marinade over the mushrooms, making sure they are well-coated. Allow them to marinate for 20-30 minutes at room temperature, turning them occasionally to distribute the marinade evenly.

4. Preheat the Grill:

· Preheat your grill to medium-high heat.

5. Grill the Portobello Mushrooms:

· Remove the marinated mushrooms from the dish or bag and shake off any excess marinade.
· Place the portobello mushroom caps on the preheated grill, gill side down.
· Grill for about 4-5 minutes on each side, or until the mushrooms are tender and have grill marks.

6. Serve:

· Remove the grilled portobello mushrooms from the grill and let them rest for a minute.

7. Assemble and Enjoy:

· You can serve the grilled portobello mushrooms in buns like a burger or as a lettuce wrap if you prefer a low-carb option.
· Add your favorite burger toppings, such as lettuce, tomato, onion, cheese, or any condiments you like.
·]Serve your grilled portobello mushrooms hot as a satisfy- ing and meaty vegetarian option.

These grilled portobello mushrooms make for a hearty and flavorful vegetarian dish that's perfect for grilling season. They are versatile and can be customized with your favorite toppings and condiments to create a delicious and satisfying meal

Garlic Butter Grilled Mushrooms

Preparation Time: 10 min | Grilling Time: 10-15 min
Servings: 4

Ingredients:

- 1 pound (450g) button mushrooms, cleaned and trimmed
- 3 tablespoons unsalted butter, melted
- 3 cloves garlic, minced
- 2 tablespoons fresh parsley, chopped
- Salt and freshly ground black pepper to taste
- 1 tablespoon lemon juice (optional, for added freshness)

Instructions:

1. Preheat the Grill:

- Preheat your grill to medium-high heat (about 400- 450°F or 200-230°C).

2. Prepare the Mushrooms:

- Clean the button mushrooms by wiping them with a damp cloth or paper towel to remove any dirt.
- Trim the tough ends of the mushroom stems if necessary. Leave smaller mushrooms whole and halve or quarter larger ones for even grilling.

3. Make Garlic Butter Sauce:

- In a small saucepan or microwave-safe bowl, melt the butter over low heat. Add the minced garlic and cook for about 1-2 minutes until fragrant. Be careful not to brown the garlic.
- Stir in the chopped fresh parsley and season the garlic butter sauce with salt and freshly ground black pepper to taste. If desired, add a tablespoon of lemon juice for extra flavor and freshness.

4. Grill the Mushrooms:

- Thread the cleaned and trimmed mushrooms onto skew- ers or use a grill basket to prevent them from falling through the grates.
- Brush the garlic butter sauce generously over the mush- rooms, coating them evenly.

5. Grill:

- Place the mushroom skewers or grill basket on the pre- heated grill. Grill for 10-15 minutes, turning occasionally until the mushrooms are tender and have a nice grill marks.

6. Serve:

- Once the mushrooms are grilled to perfection, remove them from the grill and transfer them to a serving platter.
- If you have any remaining garlic butter sauce, you can drizzle it over the grilled mushrooms for extra flavor.

7. Enjoy:

- Serve your Garlic Butter Grilled Mushrooms as a delectable side dish or appetizer. They are bursting with savory garlic and buttery goodness and make a fantastic accompaniment to grilled meats or as a topping for steaks.

These Garlic Butter Grilled Mushrooms are a mouthwatering treat for mushroom lovers and a fantastic addition to your outdoor grilling menu. Enjoy their rich, savory flavors with a hint of garlic and buttery goodness!

Smoked Cornbread

Preparation Time: 15 min | Smoking Time: 30-40 min
Servings: 8-10

Ingredients:

- 1 cup cornmeal
- 1 cup all-purpose flour
- 1/4 cup granulated sugar (adjust to taste)
- 1 tablespoon baking powder
- 1/2 teaspoon salt
- 1 cup buttermilk (or substitute with 1 cup milk mixed with 1 tablespoon white vinegar or lemon juice)
- 1/2 cup unsalted butter, melted and cooled
- 2 large eggs
- 1 cup shredded sharp cheddar cheese
- 2-3 jalapeño peppers, seeds removed and finely chopped (optional, for added flavor)
- Cooking spray or butter for greasing the pan

Instructions:

1. Preheat the Smoker:

- Preheat your smoker to 275°F (135°C) using your choice of wood chips (hickory, apple, or cherry wood are great options) for added smoky flavor.

2. Prepare the Cast Iron Skillet:

- Grease a 9x9-inch (23x23 cm) cast iron skillet or a similar- sized oven-safe pan with cooking spray or butter.

3. Prepare the Dry Ingredients:

- In a mixing bowl, combine the cornmeal, all-purpose flour, granulated sugar, baking powder, and salt. Mix well to combine.

4. Combine Wet Ingredients:

- In another bowl, whisk together the buttermilk, melted butter, and eggs until well combined.

5. Combine Wet and Dry Ingredients:

- Pour the wet ingredients into the bowl with the dry ingredients. Stir until just combined. Be careful not to overmix; a few lumps are okay.

6. Add Cheese and Jalapeños:

- Fold in the shredded cheddar cheese and finely chopped jalapeño peppers into the batter. Adjust the amount of jalapeños to your desired level of spiciness.

7. Transfer to the Smoker:

- Pour the cornbread batter into the greased cast iron skillet or pan.

8. Smoke the Cornbread:

- Place the cast iron skillet in the preheated smoker and smoke for 30-40 minutes or until the cornbread is set and a toothpick inserted into the center comes out clean.

9. Cool and Serve:

- Allow the smoked cornbread to cool in the skillet for a few minutes.
- Cut it into squares or wedges, and serve your Smoked Cornbread with a unique smoky flavor alongside your favorite smoked meats or as a tasty side dish.

Smoking cornbread adds a wonderful depth of flavor to this Southern classic. Enjoy the rich, smoky notes that complement the sweetness of the cornbread. It's perfect for barbecue gatherings and outdoor cooking adventures.

Grilled Cheddar Jalapeño Cornbread

Preparation Time: 15 min | Grilling Time: 15-20 min

Servings: 8-10

Ingredients:

- 1 cup cornmeal
- 1 cup all-purpose flour
- 1/4 cup granulated sugar (adjust to taste)
- 1 tablespoon baking powder
- 1/2 teaspoon salt
- 1 cup buttermilk (or substitute with 1 cup milk mixed with 1 tablespoon white vinegar or lemon juice)
- 1/2 cup unsalted butter, melted and cooled
- 2 large eggs
- 1 cup shredded sharp cheddar cheese
- 2-3 jalapeño peppers, seeds removed and finely chopped (optional, for added flavor)
- Cooking spray or oil for greasing the grill grates

Instructions:

1. Preheat the Grill:

- Preheat your grill to medium-high heat, targeting a temperature of around 350°F to 375°F (175°C to 190°C). Ensure that the grill grates are clean.

2. Prepare a Cast Iron Skillet:

- Grease a 9x9-inch (23x23 cm) cast iron skillet or a similar- sized oven-safe pan with cooking spray or a small amount of oil.

3. Prepare the Dry Ingredients:

- In a mixing bowl, combine the cornmeal, all-purpose flour, granulated sugar, baking powder, and salt. Mix well to combine.

4. Combine Wet Ingredients:

- In another bowl, whisk together the buttermilk, melted butter, and eggs until well combined.

5. Combine Wet and Dry Ingredients:

- Pour the wet ingredients into the bowl with the dry ingredients. Stir until just combined. Avoid overmixing; a few lumps are okay.

6. Add Cheese and Jalapeños:

- Fold in the shredded cheddar cheese and finely chopped jalapeño peppers into the batter. Adjust the amount of jalapeños to your desired level of spiciness.

7. Transfer to the Skillet:

- Pour the cornbread batter into the greased cast iron skillet.

8. Grill the Cornbread:

- Place the cast iron skillet directly on the grill grates.
- Grill the cornbread for 15-20 minutes or until it's set, golden brown on top, and a toothpick inserted into the center comes out clean.

9. Cool and Serve:

- Allow the grilled cheddar jalapeño cornbread to cool in the skillet for a few minutes.
- Cut it into squares or wedges, and serve your Grilled Cornbread with smoky flavors alongside your favorite grilled meats or as a delicious side dish.

Grilling cornbread gives it a delightful smoky char and en- hances its flavor. This recipe is perfect for outdoor barbecues and cookouts, adding a unique twist to your cornbread. Enjoy the combination of smoky, cheesy, and slightly spicy good- ness!

Grilled Garlic Bre

Prep Time: 10 min | Grilling Time: 5-7 min | Total Time: 15-17 min
Servings: 4

Ingredients:

- 1 large baguette or Italian loaf, cut in half lengthwise
- 1/2 cup (1 stick) unsalted butter, softened
- 4 cloves garlic, minced
- 2 tablespoons fresh parsley, finely chopped (optional)
- Salt and black pepper, to taste

Instructions:

1. Preheat the Grill:

- Preheat your grill to medium-high heat (about 350-400°F or 175-200°C).

2. Prepare the Garlic Butter:

- In a small mixing bowl, combine the softened butter, minced garlic, chopped fresh parsley (if using), salt, and black pepper. Mix until the ingredients are well incorporated.

3. Slice the Bread:

- Cut the baguette or Italian loaf in half lengthwise to create two long pieces of bread.

4. Butter the Bread:

- Spread the garlic butter mixture evenly over the cut sides of each bread half.

5. Grill the Garlic Bread:

- Place the garlic bread halves, cut side down, directly on the grill grates.
- Grill for about 2-3 minutes, or until the bread is toasted and has grill marks. Keep an eye on it to prevent burning.

6. Serve:

- Remove the grilled garlic bread from the grill and place it on a cutting board.
- Slice the bread into individual portions.

7. Enjoy:

- Serve your grilled garlic bread as a flavorful side dish for grilled meats, pasta, salads, or as an appetizer. It's perfect for soaking up sauces and adding a delicious garlicky kick to your meal.

Grilled garlic bread is a simple yet satisfying accompaniment to many dishes. The grill adds a smoky and charred flavor to the buttery garlic bread, making it a crowd-pleasing addition to your outdoor meals and gatherings.

Grilled Polenta with Roasted Pepper Sauce

Preparation Time: 15 min | Cooking Time: 20-25 min
Servings: 4

Ingredients:
For the Grilled Polenta:

- 1 tube (18 ounces) pre-cooked polenta (found in the grocery store)
- Olive oil for brushing
- Salt and freshly ground black pepper, to taste
- Fresh basil leaves (for garnish, optional) For the Roasted Pepper Sauce:
- 2 large red bell peppers
- 2 cloves garlic, minced
- 2 tablespoons olive oil
- 1/4 cup fresh basil leaves, packed
- 1/4 cup grated Parmesan cheese
- Salt and freshly ground black pepper, to taste

Instructions:
Preparing the Roasted Pepper Sauce:

1. Roast the Red Bell Peppers:

- Preheat your grill to high heat, around 450-500°F (232- 260°C).
- Place the red bell peppers directly on the grill grates.
- Grill for about 15-20 minutes, turning occasionally, until the peppers are charred on all sides.

2. Transfer to a Bowl:

- Remove the grilled peppers from the grill and place them in a bowl.
- Cover the bowl with plastic wrap or a kitchen towel and let the peppers steam for about 10 minutes. This will make it easier to remove the skin.

3. Peel and Remove Seeds:

- After steaming, peel off the charred skin from the peppers and remove the seeds and membranes.

4. Blend the Sauce:

- In a blender or food processor, combine the roasted red bell peppers, minced garlic, olive oil, fresh basil leaves, grated Parmesan cheese, salt, and freshly ground black pepper.
- Blend until you achieve a smooth and flavorful roasted pepper sauce.

5. Set the Sauce Aside:

· Transfer the roasted pepper sauce to a bowl and set it aside.

Grilling the Polenta:

1. Prepare the Polenta:

· Slice the pre-cooked polenta into 1/2-inch thick rounds.

2. Brush with Olive Oil:

· Brush both sides of the polenta slices lightly with olive oil.

3. Season with Salt and Pepper:

· Season the polenta slices with a pinch of salt and freshly ground black pepper to taste.

4. Grill the Polenta:

· Place the seasoned polenta slices on the preheated grill grates.

5. Grill for 3-4 Minutes per Side:

· Grill the polenta slices for about 3-4 minutes per side, or until they have grill marks and are crispy on the outside.

Serving Grilled Polenta with Roasted Pepper Sauce:

1. Plate the Polenta:

· Transfer the grilled polenta slices to a serving platter.

2. Top with Roasted Pepper Sauce:

· Spoon the prepared roasted pepper sauce generously over the grilled polenta slices.

3. Garnish and Serve:

· Garnish with fresh basil leaves, if desired.

Enjoy your Grilled Polenta with Roasted Pepper Sauce as an appetizer or side dish. The crispy grilled polenta pairs perfectly with the flavorful roasted red pepper sauce, making it a delightful and savory treat.

Grilled Avocado with Salsa

Prep Time: 10 min | Grilling Time: 5-7 min | Total Time: 15-17 min

Servings: 4

Ingredients:

For the Grilled Avocado:

- 2 ripe avocados, cut in half and pitted
- Olive oil, for brushing
- Salt and black pepper, to taste
- 1 lemon, cut into wedges (for drizzling over grilled avoca- dos)

For the Tomato Salsa:

- 2 large tomatoes, diced
- 1/2 red onion, finely chopped
- 1/4 cup fresh cilantro, chopped
- 1 jalapeño pepper, seeded and finely chopped (adjust to taste)
- 2 cloves garlic, minced
- Juice of 1 lime
- Salt and black pepper, to taste

Instructions:

1. Preheat the Grill:

- Preheat your grill to medium-high heat (about 350-400°F or 175-200°C).

2. Prepare the Tomato Salsa:

- In a bowl, combine the diced tomatoes, chopped red onion, chopped cilantro, finely chopped jalapeño pepper, minced garlic, lime juice, salt, and black pepper. Mix well to create the salsa. Adjust the seasoning and spiciness to your taste.
- Cover the salsa and refrigerate while you grill the avocados.

3. Grill the Avocado:

- Cut the ripe avocados in half and remove the pits.
- Brush the cut sides of the avocado halves lightly with olive oil to prevent sticking.
- Place the avocado halves, cut side down, directly on the grill grates.
- Grill for about 2-3 minutes, or until the avocados have grill marks and are slightly softened.

4. Serve:

- Remove the grilled avocado halves from the grill and place them on a serving platter, cut side up.
- Squeeze a little lemon juice over each grilled avocado half to enhance the flavor.

5. Top with Salsa:

- Spoon the prepared tomato salsa generously over the grilled avocado halves.

6. Enjoy:

- Serve your grilled avocado with salsa immediately as a tasty and healthy appetizer or side dish. It's a refreshing and flavorful combination of smoky, creamy avocados and zesty tomato salsa.

Grilled avocado with salsa is a delightful dish that can be served as an appetizer, side dish, or even a light and healthy snack. The combination of smoky grilled avocados and fresh tomato salsa creates a burst of flavors and textures that is sure to impress your taste buds.

Grilled Asparagus with Lemon Zest

Preparation Time: 10 min | Grilling Time: 5-7 min

Servings: 4

Ingredients:

- 1 bunch of fresh asparagus spears
- 2 tablespoons extra-virgin olive oil
- Salt and freshly ground black pepper to taste
- Zest of 1 lemon
- 1/4 cup grated Parmesan cheese (optional, for garnish)

Instructions:

1. Preheat the Grill:

2. Preheat your grill to medium-high heat. Make sure the grill grates are clean and well-oiled to prevent sticking.

3. Prepare the Asparagus:

- Wash the asparagus and trim off the tough woody ends. You can do this by snapping the asparagus where it naturally breaks or by using a knife as a guide.

4. Season the Asparagus:

- In a large mixing bowl, toss the asparagus spears with the extra-virgin olive oil, ensuring they are evenly coated.
- Season the asparagus with salt and freshly ground black pepper to taste. You can also add a touch of garlic powder or your favorite seasonings for extra flavor if desired.

5. Grill the Asparagus:

- Place the asparagus spears directly on the preheated grill grates.
- Grill the asparagus for about 5-7 minutes, turning occa- sionally, until they become tender and have grill marks. The cooking time may vary depending on the thickness of the asparagus, so keep an eye on them.

6. Zest the Lemon:

- While the asparagus is grilling, use a zester or a fine grater to zest the lemon. Set the lemon zest aside.

7. Serve:

- Once the grilled asparagus is done, transfer it to a serving platter.
- Sprinkle the freshly grated Parmesan cheese (if using) evenly over the grilled asparagus.

8. Finish with Lemon Zest:

- Before serving, generously sprinkle the lemon zest over the asparagus for a burst of fresh citrus flavor.

9. Serve Warm:

- Serve the Grilled Asparagus with Lemon Zest immediately while it's still warm.

This Grilled Asparagus with Lemon Zest is a simple yet elegant side dish that pairs well with various main courses. The smoky grilled asparagus combined with the bright and zesty lemon flavor creates a wonderful balance of tastes. Enjoy this delicious and healthy dish!

Smoky Grilled Caesar Salad

Preparation Time: 15 min | Grilling Time: 5 min

Servings: 4

Ingredients:

For the Grilled Romaine:

- 2 large heads of romaine lettuce, washed and halved lengthwise
- 1 tablespoon olive oil
- Salt and freshly ground black pepper to taste

For the Caesar Dressing:

- 1/2 cup mayonnaise
- 2 tablespoons grated Parmesan cheese
- 2 tablespoons freshly squeezed lemon juice
- 2 cloves garlic, minced
- 1 teaspoon Dijon mustard
- 1 teaspoon Worcestershire sauce
- Salt and freshly ground black pepper to taste

For Topping:

- 1/2 cup croutons
- 1/4 cup grated Parmesan cheese
- Lemon wedges for garnish (optional)

Instructions:

1. Prepare the Caesar Dressing:

- In a small bowl, whisk together the mayonnaise, grated Parmesan cheese, freshly squeezed lemon juice, minced garlic, Dijon mustard, Worcestershire sauce, salt, and freshly ground black pepper. Taste and adjust the sea- soning if needed. Refrigerate the dressing until ready to use.

2. Preheat the Grill:

- Preheat your grill to medium-high heat.

3. Grill the Romaine Lettuce:

- Brush the cut sides of the romaine lettuce halves with olive oil and season them with salt and freshly ground black pepper.
- Place the romaine halves on the preheated grill, cut side down.
- Grill for about 2-3 minutes until you get grill marks and the lettuce is slightly charred. Be careful not to overcook; you want the lettuce to remain crisp and smoky.

4. Assemble the Salad:

- Arrange the grilled romaine halves on a serving platter or individual plates, cut side up.

5. Dress the Salad:

- Drizzle the Caesar dressing generously over the grilled romaine lettuce.

6. Add Toppings:

- Sprinkle croutons evenly over the dressed lettuce.
- Top the salad with grated Parmesan cheese.

7. Garnish (Optional):

- Garnish the Smoky Grilled Caesar Salad with lemon wedges for an extra burst of citrus flavor.

8. Serve:

- Serve the salad immediately while the romaine is still warm and smoky.

This Smoky Grilled Caesar Salad is a creative twist on the classic Caesar salad, adding a wonderful smoky flavor to the crisp romaine. Enjoy the combination of charred lettuce, creamy dressing, crunchy croutons, and savory Parmesan cheese!

Grilled Peach and Arugula Salad

Preparation Time: 15 min | Grilling Time: 5 min

Servings: 4

Ingredients:

For the Salad:

- 4 ripe peaches, halved and pitted
- 6 cups fresh arugula
- 1/2 cup crumbled goat cheese or feta cheese
- 1/4 cup chopped toasted pecans or walnuts (optional, for garnish)

For the Vinaigrette:

- 3 tablespoons extra-virgin olive oil
- 2 tablespoons balsamic vinegar
- 1 tablespoon honey
- 1 teaspoon Dijon mustard
- Salt and freshly ground black pepper to taste

Instructions:

1. Preheat the Grill:

- Preheat your grill to medium-high heat.

2. Prepare the Vinaigrette:

- In a small bowl, whisk together the extra-virgin olive oil, balsamic vinegar, honey, Dijon mustard, salt, and freshly ground black pepper until well combined. Set aside.

3. Grill the Peaches:

- Brush the cut sides of the peach halves with a little olive oil to prevent sticking.
- Place the peach halves on the preheated grill, cut side down.
- Grill for about 2-3 minutes, or until grill marks form and the peaches are slightly caramelized. You want them to be warm but not overly soft.

4. Assemble the Salad:

- Arrange the fresh arugula on a serving platter or individ- ual plates.

5. Add Grilled Peaches:

- Place the grilled peach halves, cut side up, over the bed of arugula.

6. Drizzle with Vinaigrette:

- Drizzle the prepared vinaigrette over the grilled peaches and arugula.

7. Add Cheese and Nuts:

- Sprinkle crumbled goat cheese or feta cheese over the salad.
- Optionally, sprinkle chopped toasted pecans or walnuts over the top for added crunch and flavor.

8. Serve:

- Serve the Grilled Peach and Arugula Salad immediately as an appetizer or side dish.

This Grilled Peach and Arugula Salad is a delightful combina- tion of sweet, smoky grilled peaches and peppery arugula, all brought together by a light and tangy vinaigrette. It's perfect for summer gatherings and pairs beautifully with grilled meats. Enjoy!

Grilled Pineapple with Cinnamon Honey Drizzle

Prep Time: 10 min | Grilling Time: 6-8 min | Total Time: 16-18 min
Servings: 4

Ingredients:
For the Grilled Pineapple:

- 1 whole pineapple, peeled, cored, and sliced into rings or spears
- Cooking spray or vegetable oil for brushing

For the Cinnamon Honey Drizzle:

- 1/4 cup honey
- 1 teaspoon ground cinnamon
- 1 tablespoon fresh lime juice (optional)
- Fresh mint leaves, for garnish (optional)

Instructions:

1. Preheat the Grill:

- Preheat your grill to medium-high heat.

2. Prepare the Cinnamon Honey Drizzle:

- In a small bowl, whisk together the honey, ground cin- namon, and fresh lime juice (if using). Mix until the cinnamon is fully incorporated into the honey. Set aside.

3. Grill the Pineapple:

- Lightly grease the grill grates with cooking spray or vegetable oil to prevent sticking.
- Place the pineapple rings or spears directly on the pre- heated grill.
- Grill for approximately 3-4 minutes on each side, or until the pineapple has grill marks and is slightly caramelized. The total grilling time may vary depending on the thick- ness of your pineapple slices.

4. Serve:

- Remove the grilled pineapple from the grill and arrange them on a serving platter.

5. Drizzle with Cinnamon Honey:

- Drizzle the prepared cinnamon honey mixture over the grilled pineapple slices.

6. Garnish:

- Optionally, garnish with fresh mint leaves for a burst of color and flavor.

7. Enjoy:

- Serve your grilled pineapple with cinnamon honey drizzle as a delectable and refreshing dessert, side dish, or a light and healthy snack.

Grilled pineapple with cinnamon honey drizzle is a delightful combination of smoky, caramelized pineapple and sweet, aromatic cinnamon honey. It's a simple yet elegant treat that's perfect for warm weather gatherings or a sweet ending to a barbecue meal.

Applewood Smoked Cheddar

Preparation Time: 15 min | Smoking Time: 1-2 hours
Servings: Varies

Ingredients:

- 1 block of aged cheddar cheese (8-16 ounces), preferably a sharp or extra sharp variety
- Applewood chips or chunks for smoking

Equipment:

- Smoker
- Cold smoking attachment (if your smoker doesn't have a cold smoking feature)

Instructions:

Preparing the Cheese:

1. Select the Cheese: Choose a block of aged cheddar cheese with a flavor profile you enjoy. Sharp or extra sharp cheddar works well because it can stand up to the smoky flavor.
2. Cut the Cheese: Cut the block of cheddar cheese into smaller pieces or chunks. You can leave the cheese block whole if you prefer, but smaller pieces allow for more surface area to absorb the smoky flavor.

Preparing the Smoker:

1. Preheat the Smoker: Preheat your smoker to the cold smoking temperature, which is typically around 90-100°F (32-37°C). If your smoker doesn't have a cold smoking feature, you can use a cold smoking attachment or a smoking tube.
2. Soak the Wood Chips: While the smoker is preheating, soak the applewood chips or chunks in water for about 30 minutes. Drain them before using.

Smoking the Cheddar:

1. Place the Cheese: Place the chunks or pieces of cheddar cheese on a wire rack or a smoking tray inside the smoker. Ensure there is some space between the cheese pieces for the smoke to circulate.

2. Add the Wood Chips: If you're using a smoker with a cold smoking feature, add the soaked applewood chips to the smoker's wood chip tray. If not, place the smoking tube filled with the wood chips near the cheese.

3. Smoke the Cheese: Close the smoker and smoke the cheddar cheese at the cold smoking temperature (around 90-100°F or 32-37°C) for 1-2 hours. The longer you smoke it, the stronger the smoky flavor will be, so adjust the time to your taste preference.

Resting and Storing:

1. Cool and Rest: Once the smoking time is complete, remove the smoked cheddar from the smoker and allow it to cool to room temperature. It's essential to let it rest for a few hours to allow the smoky flavor to mellow and distribute evenly.

2. Wrap and Refrigerate: Wrap the smoked cheddar in plastic wrap or wax paper and refrigerate it for at least 24 hours or up to a few days. This resting period allows the smoky flavor to meld with the cheese.

Serving:

1. Enjoy: After the resting period, your Applewood Smoked Cheddar is ready to be enjoyed. Serve it on a cheese board with crackers, fresh fruit, and perhaps a glass of wine for a delightful and smoky cheese experience.

Applewood Smoked Cheddar adds a subtle, sweet smokiness to your cheese platter, making it a perfect appetizer or snack for gatherings or special occasions. Feel free to experiment with different cheese varieties and smoking times to achieve your preferred level of smokiness.

Hickory Smoked Gouda

Preparation Time: 15 min | Smoking Time: 1-2 hours
Servings: Varies

Ingredients:

- 1 block of Gouda cheese (8-16 ounces), preferably aged Gouda
- Hickory wood chips or chunks for smoking

Equipment:

- Smoker
- Cold smoking attachment (if your smoker doesn't have a cold smoking feature)

Instructions:

Preparing the Cheese:

1. Select the Gouda: Choose a block of Gouda cheese, preferably aged Gouda, as it has a more robust flavor that pairs well with the smokiness. You can choose the size of the block based on your preferences.
2. Cut the Cheese: Cut the Gouda cheese into smaller pieces or chunks. You can leave the cheese block whole, but smaller pieces allow for more surface area to absorb the smoky flavor.

Preparing the Smoker:

1. Preheat the Smoker: Preheat your smoker to the cold smoking temperature, which is typically around 90-100°F (32-37°C). If your smoker doesn't have a cold smoking feature, you can use a cold smoking attachment or a smoking tube.
2. Soak the Wood Chips: While the smoker is preheating, soak the hickory wood chips or chunks in water for about 30 minutes. Drain them before using.

Smoking the Gouda:

1. Place the Cheese: Place the chunks or pieces of Gouda cheese on a wire rack or a smoking tray inside the smoker. Ensure there is some space between the cheese pieces for the smoke to circulate.

2. Add the Wood Chips: If you're using a smoker with a cold smoking feature, add the soaked hickory wood chips to the smoker's wood chip tray. If not, place the smoking tube filled with the wood chips near the cheese.

3. Smoke the Cheese: Close the smoker and smoke the Gouda cheese at the cold smoking temperature (around 90-100°F or 32-37°C) for 1-2 hours. The longer you smoke it, the stronger the hickory smoky flavor will be, so adjust the time to your taste preference.

Resting and Storing:

1. Cool and Rest: Once the smoking time is complete, remove the smoked Gouda from the smoker and allow it to cool to room temperature. Let it rest for a few hours to allow the smoky flavor to mellow and distribute evenly.

2. Wrap and Refrigerate: Wrap the smoked Gouda in plastic wrap or wax paper and refrigerate it for at least 24 hours or up to a few days. This resting period allows the smoky flavor to meld with the cheese.

Serving:

1. Enjoy: After the resting period, your Hickory Smoked Gouda is ready to be enjoyed. Slice it and serve it on a cheese platter, use it for sandwiches, or melt it into dishes for a rich, smoky flavor.

Hickory Smoked Gouda offers a hearty, smoky twist to this beloved cheese, making it a versatile addition to your culinary creations. Whether you enjoy it on its own or use it in various recipes, the rich smokiness will elevate your dishes.

Smoked Mozzarella with Herbs

Preparation Time: 15 min | Smoking Time: 1-2 hours
Servings: Varies

Ingredients:

- 1 ball of fresh mozzarella (8-16 ounces)
- Olive oil for brushing
- 2 tablespoons fresh basil, chopped
- 1 tablespoon fresh rosemary, chopped
- 1 tablespoon fresh thyme leaves
- 1 teaspoon dried oregano
- 1 teaspoon dried red pepper flakes (optional for a hint of spice)
- Salt and black pepper to taste

Equipment:

- Smoker
- Cold smoking attachment (if your smoker doesn't have a cold smoking feature)

Instructions:

Preparing the Mozzarella:

1. Select the Mozzarella: Choose a fresh mozzarella ball, and the size can vary based on your preferences. The mozzarella should be relatively firm to withstand the smoking process.

2. Cut the Mozzarella: Cut the fresh mozzarella into smaller pieces or slices. Smaller pieces allow for more surface area to absorb the smoky flavor.

Preparing the Herb Mix:

1. Create the Herb Mix: In a bowl, combine chopped fresh basil, fresh rosemary, fresh thyme leaves, dried oregano, and dried red pepper flakes (if using). Season with salt and black pepper to taste. Mix well to create the herb mixture.

Preparing the Smoker:

1. Preheat the Smoker: Preheat your smoker to the cold smoking temperature, which is typically around 90-100°F (32-37°C). If your smoker doesn't have a cold smoking feature, you can use a cold smoking attachment or a smoking tube.

2. Soak the Wood Chips: While the smoker is preheating, soak wood chips (such as apple or cherry) in water for about 30 minutes. Drain them before using.

Smoking the Mozzarella:

1. Brush with Olive Oil: Brush the slices or pieces of fresh mozzarella lightly with olive oil to prevent sticking during smoking.

2. Place the Cheese: Arrange the prepared mozzarella pieces on a wire rack or a smoking tray inside the smoker. Ensure they are well-spaced for even smoking.

3. Add the Wood Chips: If you're using a smoker with a cold smoking feature, add the soaked wood chips to the smoker's wood chip tray. If not, place the smoking tube filled with the wood chips near the cheese.

4. Smoke the Cheese: Close the smoker and smoke the mozzarella at the cold smoking temperature (around 90-100°F or 32-37°C) for 1-2 hours. The longer you smoke it, the stronger the smoky flavor will be, so adjust the time to your taste preference.

Resting and Serving:

1. Cool and Rest: Once the smoking time is complete, remove the smoked mozzarella from the smoker and allow it to cool to room temperature. Let it rest for a few hours to allow the smoky flavor to mellow and blend with the herbs.

2. Serve: Your Smoked Mozzarella with Herbs is now ready to be enjoyed. Serve it on a salad, as an appetizer with crusty bread, or incorporate it into your favorite dishes for a delightful smoky and herby flavor.

Smoked Mozzarella with Herbs is a versatile ingredient that adds a smoky and herbaceous dimension to your culinary creations. Its creamy texture and rich flavor make it a delightful addition to various dishes and appetizers.

Maple Smoked Brie

Preparation Time: 15 min | Smoking Time: 1-2 hours
Servings: Varies

Ingredients:

- 1 wheel of brie cheese (8-16 ounces), preferably ripe but not overly runny
- Maple wood chips for smoking

Equipment:

- Smoker
- Cold smoking attachment (if your smoker doesn't have a cold smoking feature)

Instructions:

Preparing the Brie:

1. Select the Brie: Choose a wheel of brie cheese that is ripe but not overly runny. The size of the wheel can vary based on your preferences.
2. Score the Brie: Use a knife to gently score the top of the brie cheese in a crisscross pattern. This will allow the smoky flavor to penetrate the cheese.

Preparing the Smoker:

1. Preheat the Smoker: Preheat your smoker to the cold smoking temperature, which is typically around 90-100°F (32-37°C). If your smoker doesn't have a cold smoking feature, you can use a cold smoking attachment or a smoking tube.
2. Soak the Wood Chips: While the smoker is preheating, soak the maple wood chips in water for about 30 minutes. Drain them before using.

Smoking the Brie:

1. Place the Brie: Place the scored wheel of brie cheese on a wire rack or a smoking tray inside the smoker. Ensure there is some space around the cheese for the smoke to circulate.

2. Add the Wood Chips: If you're using a smoker with a cold smoking feature, add the soaked maple wood chips to the smoker's wood chip tray. If not, place the smoking tube filled with the wood chips near the cheese.

3. Smoke the Brie: Close the smoker and smoke the brie cheese at the cold smoking temperature (around 90-100°F or 32-37°C) for 1-2 hours. The longer you smoke it, the stronger the maple smoky flavor will be, so adjust the time to your taste preference.

Resting and Serving:

1. Cool and Rest: Once the smoking time is complete, remove the smoked brie from the smoker and allow it to cool to room temperature. Let it rest for a few hours to allow the smoky flavor to mellow and blend with the creamy cheese.

2. Serve: Your Maple Smoked Brie is now ready to be enjoyed. Serve it with crackers, crusty bread, fresh fruit, or a drizzle of honey for a delightful sweet and smoky cheese experience.

Maple Smoked Brie combines the creaminess of brie with the unique sweet and smoky flavor of maple wood. It's a perfect addition to cheese platters, appetizers, or as a special treat for cheese enthusiasts.

Smoked Blue Cheese

Preparation Time: 15 min | Smoking Time: 1-2 hours
Servings: Varies

Ingredients:

- 1 wedge or block of blue cheese (8-16 ounces)
- Your choice of smoking wood chips (such as hickory or mesquite)

Equipment:

- Smoker
- Cold smoking attachment (if your smoker doesn't have a cold smoking feature)

Instructions:

Preparing the Blue Cheese:

1. Select the Blue Cheese: Choose a wedge or block of blue cheese, and the size can vary based on your preferences. Blue cheese with a creamy texture works well for smok- ing.
2. Cut the Cheese: Cut the blue cheese into smaller pieces or chunks. Smaller pieces allow for more surface area to absorb the smoky flavor.

Preparing the Smoker:

1. Preheat the Smoker: Preheat your smoker to the cold smoking temperature, which is typically around 90- 100°F (32-37°C). If your smoker doesn't have a cold smoking feature, you can use a cold smoking attachment or a smoking tube.
2. Soak the Wood Chips: While the smoker is preheat- ing, soak the smoking wood chips (such as hickory or mesquite) in water for about 30 minutes. Drain them before using.

Smoking the Blue Cheese:

1. Place the Cheese: Arrange the prepared blue cheese pieces on a wire rack or a smoking tray inside the smoker. Ensure they are well-spaced to allow the smoke to circulate.

2. Add the Wood Chips: If you're using a smoker with a cold smoking feature, add the soaked smoking wood chips to the smoker's wood chip tray. If not, place the smoking tube filled with the wood chips near the cheese.

3. Smoke the Cheese: Close the smoker and smoke the blue cheese at the cold smoking temperature (around 90-100°F or 32-37°C) for 1-2 hours. The longer you smoke it, the more intense the smoky flavor will be, so adjust the time to your taste preference.

Resting and Serving:

1. Cool and Rest: Once the smoking time is complete, remove the smoked blue cheese from the smoker and allow it to cool to room temperature. Let it rest for a few hours to allow the smoky flavor to mellow and meld with the cheese.

2. Serve: Your Smoked Blue Cheese is now ready to be enjoyed. Crumble it over salads, use it as a topping for grilled steaks, or pair it with crackers and fresh fruit for a delectable appetizer.

Smoked Blue Cheese adds a bold and smoky dimension to your dishes. Its pungent flavor and creamy texture make it a versatile ingredient for various culinary creations.

Smoked Provolone with Garlic

Preparation Time: 15 min | Smoking Time: 1-2 hours
Servings: Varies

Ingredients:

- 1 block or wedge of provolone cheese (8-16 ounces)
- 2-3 cloves of garlic, minced
- Olive oil for brushing

Equipment:

- Smoker
- Cold smoking attachment (if your smoker doesn't have a cold smoking feature)

Instructions:

Preparing the Provolone:

1. Select the Provolone: Choose a block or wedge of pro- volone cheese with a mild, creamy taste. The size can vary based on your preferences.
2. Mince the Garlic: Finely mince 2-3 cloves of garlic, or adjust the amount to your taste preference.

Preparing the Smoker:

1. Preheat the Smoker: Preheat your smoker to the cold smoking temperature, which is typically around 90-100°F (32-37°C). If your smoker doesn't have a cold smoking feature, you can use a cold smoking attachment or a smoking tube.
2. Soak the Wood Chips: While the smoker is preheating, soak the wood chips (such as apple or cherry) in water for about 30 minutes. Drain them before using.

Smoking the Provolone:

1. Brush with Olive Oil: Brush the block or wedge of provolone cheese lightly with olive oil. This will help the garlic adhere to the cheese and prevent sticking during smoking.

2. Apply the Garlic: Sprinkle the minced garlic evenly over the surface of the provolone cheese. Gently press the garlic into the cheese to ensure it adheres.

3. Place the Cheese: Place the prepared provolone cheese on a wire rack or a smoking tray inside the smoker. Ensure there is some space around the cheese for the smoke to circulate.

4. Add the Wood Chips: If you're using a smoker with a cold smoking feature, add the soaked wood chips to the smoker's wood chip tray. If not, place the smoking tube filled with the wood chips near the cheese.

5. Smoke the Cheese: Close the smoker and smoke the pro- volone cheese at the cold smoking temperature (around 90-100°F or 32-37°C) for 1-2 hours. The longer you smoke it, the more pronounced the smoky and garlic flavor will be, so adjust the time to your taste preference.

Resting and Serving:

1. Cool and Rest: Once the smoking time is complete, remove the smoked provolone with garlic from the smoker and allow it to cool to room temperature. Let it rest for a few hours to allow the smoky and garlic flavors to meld with the cheese.

2. Serve: Your Smoked Provolone with Garlic is now ready to be enjoyed. Serve it as part of a cheese platter, pair it with crusty bread, or use it to add depth to your favorite dishes.

Smoked Provolone with Garlic is a delightful combination of creamy cheese, smoky richness, and the savory kick of garlic. It's a versatile addition to a variety of dishes and appetizers.

Grill and Smoker Recipes

Grilling Recipes: Beef

Classic Grilled Ribeye Steak

Preparation Time: 15 min | Marinating Time: 1-2 hours (optional) | Cooking Time: 10-15 min
Servings: 2

Ingredients:

- 2 ribeye steaks (about 1 to 1.5 inches thick)
- 2 tablespoons olive oil
- 2 cloves garlic, minced
- 1 teaspoon fresh rosemary, chopped (or ½ teaspoon dried rosemary)
- 1 teaspoon fresh thyme leaves (or ½ teaspoon dried thyme)
- Salt and freshly ground black pepper, to taste

Instructions:

1. Preheat the Grill:

- Preheat your grill to high heat (about 450-500°F or 232-260°C) for direct grilling.

2. Prepare the Steaks:

- Take the ribeye steaks out of the refrigerator and let them sit at room temperature for about 30 minutes before grilling.
- If you have time, you can marinate the steaks. In a small bowl, combine the olive oil, minced garlic, chopped rosemary, thyme, salt, and black pepper. Rub this mixture over both sides of the steaks and let them marinate in the refrigerator for 1-2 hours.

3. Season the Steaks:

- Before grilling, season the steaks generously with salt and freshly ground black pepper. Don't be afraid to use a good amount of seasoning; ribeye steaks can handle it.

4. Grill the Steaks:

   - Place the seasoned ribeye steaks on the hot grill grates directly over the flames.
   - Grill for about 4-5 minutes on each side for medium- rare, or adjust the time according to your desired level of doneness.
   - To get those beautiful grill marks, rotate the steaks 45 degrees after a couple of minutes on each side.

5. Check for Doneness:

   - Use a meat thermometer to check the internal tempera- ture. For medium-rare, aim for an internal temperature of 130-135°F (54-57°C).
   - Keep in mind that the steak's temperature will rise a few degrees while it rests.

6. Rest the Steaks:

   - Remove the ribeye steaks from the grill and transfer them to a cutting board or plate.
   - Tent the steaks loosely with aluminum foil and let them rest for about 5-10 minutes. This resting period allows the juices to redistribute and ensures a juicy, tender steak.

7. Slice and Serve:

   - After resting, slice the ribeye steaks against the grain into ½-inch thick slices.
   - Serve your classic grilled ribeye steaks with your favorite sides, such as grilled vegetables, a baked potato, or a fresh salad.

Enjoy your perfectly grilled ribeye steak with its smoky, savory flavor, and juicy, tender interior. This timeless recipe is sure to impress both family and guests at your next barbecue or special occasion.

Garlic Butter Grilled T-Bone Steak

Preparation Time: 15 min | Marinating Time: 30 min (optional) | Cooking Time: 10-15 min Servings: 2

Ingredients:

- 2 T-bone steaks (about 1.5 to 2 inches thick)
- Salt and freshly ground black pepper, to taste For the Garlic Butter Sauce:
- 1/2 cup (1 stick) unsalted butter, softened
- 4 cloves garlic, minced
- 2 tablespoons fresh parsley, chopped
- 1 tablespoon fresh thyme leaves (or 1 teaspoon dried thyme)
- Salt and freshly ground black pepper, to taste

Instructions:

1. Preheat the Grill:

- Preheat your grill to high heat (about 450-500°F or 232-260°C) for direct grilling.

2. Prepare the T-Bone Steaks:

- Take the T-bone steaks out of the refrigerator and let them sit at room temperature for about 30 minutes before grilling.
- Season both sides of the steaks generously with salt and freshly ground black pepper.

3. Make the Garlic Butter Sauce:

- In a small bowl, combine the softened butter, minced garlic, chopped fresh parsley, fresh thyme leaves (or dried thyme), salt, and black pepper.
- Mix well to create a flavorful garlic butter sauce.

4. Marinate the Steaks (Optional):

- If you have time, you can brush the T-bone steaks with a portion of the garlic butter sauce and let them marinate for 30 minutes to an hour in the refrigerator. This enhances the flavor and tenderness.

5. Grill the T-Bone Steaks:

- Place the seasoned T-bone steaks directly on the hot grill grates over the flames.
- Grill for about 4-5 minutes on each side for medium- rare, or adjust the time according to your desired level of doneness.
- To get those appealing grill marks, rotate the steaks 45 degrees after a couple of minutes on each side.

6. Baste with Garlic Butter:

- As the steaks cook, baste them with the remaining garlic butter sauce. Use a brush to apply the sauce generously to both sides.

7. Check for Doneness:

- Use a meat thermometer to check the internal tempera- ture. For medium-rare, aim for an internal temperature of 130-135°F (54-57°C).
- Keep in mind that the steak's temperature will rise a few degrees while it rests.

8. Rest the Steaks:

- Remove the T-bone steaks from the grill and transfer them to a cutting board or plate.
- Tent the steaks loosely with aluminum foil and let them rest for about 5-10 minutes. This resting period allows the juices to redistribute and ensures a juicy, tender steak.

9. Slice and Serve:

- After resting, slice the T-bone steaks, separating the tenderloin and strip steak sections.
- Serve your Garlic Butter Grilled T-Bone Steaks hot with additional garlic butter sauce on top.

Enjoy the rich and savory flavors of these Garlic Butter Grilled T-Bone Steaks, which are sure to impress your family and guests. The garlic butter basting adds a delightful layer of richness to the already delicious T-bone steak, making it a mouthwatering treat for any special occasion or barbecue gathering.

Chimichurri Grilled Skirt Steak

Preparation Time: 15 min | Marinating Time: 1-2 hours (optional) | Cooking Time: 10-12 min
Servings: 4

Ingredients:
For the Skirt Steak:

- 2 pounds (about 900g) skirt steak
- 2 tablespoons olive oil
- 2 cloves garlic, minced
- 1 teaspoon smoked paprika
- 1 teaspoon ground cumin
- Salt and freshly ground black pepper, to taste For the Chimichurri Sauce:
- 1 cup fresh parsley leaves, finely chopped
- 1/4 cup fresh cilantro leaves, finely chopped
- 3 cloves garlic, minced
- 1 small red onion, finely chopped
- 1 red chili pepper, finely chopped (adjust to taste)
- 1/4 cup red wine vinegar
- 1/2 cup extra-virgin olive oil
- 1 teaspoon dried oregano
- Salt and freshly ground black pepper, to taste
- Juice of 1 lime (optional)

Instructions:
For the Skirt Steak:

1. Prepare the Skirt Steak:

- If the skirt steak is in one long piece, cut it into manage- able sections to fit on the grill.
- In a bowl, combine the olive oil, minced garlic, smoked paprika, ground cumin, salt, and black pepper to create a marinade.

2. Marinate the Steak (Optional):

- Place the skirt steak pieces in a shallow dish or resealable plastic bag.
- Pour the marinade over the steak, making sure it's well- coated.
- Seal the dish or bag and refrigerate for 1-2 hours to allow the flavors to infuse. You can skip this step if you're short on time.

116

For the Chimichurri Sauce:

1. Prepare the Chimichurri Sauce:

- In a bowl, combine the finely chopped fresh parsley, cilantro, minced garlic, chopped red onion, and red chili pepper.
- Add the red wine vinegar, extra-virgin olive oil, dried oregano, salt, and black pepper.
- Optionally, add the juice of one lime for an extra zesty kick.
- Mix all the ingredients together until well combined.
- Taste and adjust the seasoning, vinegar, or chili pepper to your preference. The sauce should be bright and flavorful.

Grilling the Skirt Steak:

1. Preheat the Grill:

- Preheat your grill to high heat, around 450-500°F (232- 260°C) for direct grilling.

2. Grill the Skirt Steak:

- Remove the skirt steak from the marinade and let any excess drip off.
- Place the steak pieces on the hot grill grates.
- Grill for about 2-3 minutes per side for medium-rare or adjust the cooking time according to your preferred level of doneness. Skirt steak is best when cooked to medium- rare or medium.

3. Rest and Slice:

- Remove the grilled skirt steak from the grill and let it rest for a few minutes to allow the juices to redistribute.
- Slice the steak against the grain into thin strips for tenderness.

Serving:

1. Serve with Chimichurri Sauce:

- Arrange the sliced skirt steak on a serving platter.
- Drizzle the fresh chimichurri sauce generously over the grilled steak.
- Serve hot with your choice of side dishes, such as grilled vegetables, rice, or a fresh salad.

Enjoy the tender and flavorful Chimichurri Grilled Skirt Steak with its South American flair. The combination of the smoky grilled steak and the zesty, herbaceous chimichurri sauce is a match made in culinary heaven and is sure to delight your taste buds.

Bourbon and Brown Sugar Marinated Steak

Preparation Time: 15 min | Marinating Time: 2-4 hours (or overnight) | Cooking Time: 10-12 min
Servings: 4

Ingredients:
For the Steak:

- 4 boneless sirloin or New York strip steaks (about 1 to 1.5 inches thick)
- 1/2 cup bourbon whiskey
- 1/4 cup brown sugar
- 1/4 cup soy sauce
- 2 cloves garlic, minced
- 1 teaspoon smoked paprika
- 1/2 teaspoon ground black pepper
- 1/2 teaspoon salt
- 1/4 teaspoon cayenne pepper (adjust to taste)

Instructions:

1. Prepare the Steak:

- Place the steaks in a large, shallow dish or a resealable plastic bag.

2. Make the Bourbon and Brown Sugar Marinade:

- In a bowl, combine the bourbon whiskey, brown sugar, soy sauce, minced garlic, smoked paprika, ground black pepper, salt, and cayenne pepper.
- Mix well until the brown sugar is dissolved and the marinade is well blended.

3. Marinate the Steak:

- Pour the marinade over the steaks, ensuring they are fully submerged.
- Seal the dish or bag and refrigerate for 2-4 hours to allow the flavors to infuse. For even more flavor, marinate overnight if possible.

4. Preheat the Grill:

- Preheat your grill to medium-high heat, around 450-500°F (232-260°C) for direct grilling.

5. Grill the Steak:

- Remove the marinated steaks from the refrigerator and let them come to room temperature for about 30 minutes.
- Place the steaks on the hot grill grates.
- Grill for about 4-6 minutes on each side for medium-rare, or adjust the cooking time according to your desired level of doneness. Ensure you flip the steaks only once during grilling.

6. Check for Doneness:

- Use a meat thermometer to check the internal tempera- ture. For medium-rare, aim for an internal temperature of 130-135°F (54-57°C).
- Remember that the steak's temperature will rise a few degrees while it rests.

7. Rest and Serve:

- Remove the Bourbon and Brown Sugar Marinated Steaks from the grill and let them rest for about 5-10 minutes on a cutting board or plate. This allows the juices to redistribute and ensures a juicy, tender steak.

8. Slice and Serve:

- After resting, slice the steaks to your desired thickness.
- Serve the marinated steak hot with your favorite side dishes, such as grilled vegetables, mashed potatoes, or a fresh salad.

Enjoy the sweet and smoky flavors of this Bourbon and Brown Sugar Marinated Steak. The combination of bourbon, brown sugar, and smoky spices creates a rich and savory profile that enhances the natural flavors of the steak. It's a perfect choice for a special grilling meal that's sure to impress.

Korean BBQ Short Ribs (Galbi/Kalbi)

Preparation Time: 30 min | Marinating Time: 2-4 hours (or overnight) | Cooking Time: 10-15 min
Servings: 4-6

Ingredients:

For the Marinade:

- 2 pounds (about 1 kg) Korean-style short ribs (beef flanken or cross-cut ribs)
- 1/2 cup soy sauce
- 1/4 cup mirin (sweet rice wine)
- 1/4 cup brown sugar
- 3 cloves garlic, minced
- 1 small onion, grated
- 2 tablespoons grated Asian pear (or substitute with apple)
- 2 tablespoons grated ginger
- 2 tablespoons sesame oil
- 1 tablespoon rice wine vinegar
- 1 teaspoon freshly ground black pepper
- 1 green onion, thinly sliced (optional, for garnish)
- Toasted sesame seeds (optional, for garnish)

Instructions:

1. Prepare the Short Ribs:

- If the short ribs are not pre-cut into individual pieces, you can ask your butcher to do so or use a cleaver to cut them between the bones. Each piece should be about 1/4 to 1/2 inch thick.
- Place the short ribs in a large bowl or a resealable plastic bag.

2. Make the Marinade:

- In a separate bowl, whisk together the soy sauce, mirin, brown sugar, minced garlic, grated onion, grated Asian pear (or apple), grated ginger, sesame oil, rice wine vinegar, and freshly ground black pepper until the sugar has dissolved.

3. Marinate the Ribs:

- Pour the marinade over the short ribs, ensuring that they are well coated.
- Seal the bowl or bag and refrigerate for 2-4 hours, or ideally overnight, to allow the flavors to meld and the meat to absorb the marinade.

4. Preheat the Grill:

- Preheat your grill to medium-high heat, around 450- 500°F (232-260°C).

5. Grill the Short Ribs:

- Remove the marinated short ribs from the refrigerator and let them come to room temperature for about 30 minutes.
- Remove excess marinade from the ribs to prevent exces- sive flare-ups on the grill.
- Place the ribs on the preheated grill grates.
- Grill for about 3-4 minutes on each side or until they are nicely charred and cooked to your desired level of doneness. Korean short ribs are typically cooked to medium-rare or medium.

6. Serve:

- Transfer the grilled short ribs to a serving platter.
- Garnish with thinly sliced green onions and toasted sesame seeds, if desired.
- Serve the Korean BBQ Short Ribs hot with steamed rice and your favorite banchan (Korean side dishes).

Enjoy the sweet and tangy flavors of these Korean BBQ Short Ribs, which are a delightful fusion of flavors. The marinade infuses the meat with rich, savory notes, while the grill adds a satisfying smokiness. It's a fantastic dish to enjoy with family and friends, especially at a Korean BBQ-themed meal.

Tex-Mex Style Beef Fajita Kebabs

Preparation Time: 30 min | Marinating Time: 2-4 hours | Cooking Time: 10-15 min
Servings: 4-6

Ingredients:
For the Beef Fajita Marinade:

- 1.5 pounds (680g) beef sirloin or flank steak, cut into 1- inch cubes
- 1/4 cup olive oil
- 3 cloves garlic, minced
- Juice of 2 limes
- 2 tablespoons chili powder
- 1 tablespoon ground cumin
- 1 teaspoon paprika
- 1/2 teaspoon cayenne pepper (adjust to taste)
- Salt and freshly ground black pepper, to taste For the Kebabs:
- 2 bell peppers (red, green, or yellow), cut into 1-inch pieces
- 1 large red onion, cut into 1-inch pieces
- Wooden or metal skewers (if using wooden skewers, soak them in water for 30 minutes before using)

Instructions:
For the Beef Fajita Marinade:

1. Prepare the Marinade:

- In a bowl, combine the olive oil, minced garlic, lime juice, chili powder, ground cumin, paprika, cayenne pepper, salt, and black pepper.
- Mix well to create a flavorful beef fajita marinade.

2. Marinate the Beef:

- Place the beef cubes in a large resealable plastic bag or a shallow dish.
- Pour the marinade over the beef, making sure it's well- coated.
- Seal the bag or cover the dish with plastic wrap and refrigerate for 2-4 hours, allowing the flavors to infuse and tenderize the meat. You can marinate it overnight for even more flavor.

Assembling and Grilling the Kebabs:

1. 1. Preheat the Grill:

- Preheat your grill to medium-high heat, around 450- 500°F (232-260°C) for direct grilling.

2. Assemble the Kebabs:

- Thread the marinated beef cubes onto skewers, alternat- ing with bell pepper pieces and red onion chunks to create colorful and flavorful kebabs.

3. Grill the Kebabs:

- Place the assembled beef fajita kebabs on the preheated grill grates.
- Grill for about 3-4 minutes on each side, turning occa- sionally, until the beef is cooked to your desired level of done- ness. Aim for medium-rare to medium for the best results.

4. Check for Doneness:

- Use a meat thermometer to check the internal tempera- ture. For medium-rare, aim for an internal temperature of 130-135°F (54-57°C).

5. Rest and Serve:

- Remove the beef fajita kebabs from the grill and let them rest for about 5 minutes on a serving platter. This allows the juices to redistribute and ensures a juicy, tender result.

6. Serve:

- Serve the Tex-Mex Style Beef Fajita Kebabs hot with warm tortillas, salsa, guacamole, sour cream, and any other Tex-Mex toppings you prefer.

Enjoy these flavorful and colorful Tex-Mex Style Beef Fajita Kebabs, perfect for a Tex-Mex-themed cookout or a fun outdoor meal with family and friends. The marinated beef, combined with bell peppers and onions, delivers a burst of Tex-Mex flavors that will satisfy your taste buds.

Spicy Beef Kebabs

Preparation Time: 20 min | Marinating Time: 2-4 hours | Cooking Time: 10-15 min
Servings: 4

Ingredients:

For the Marinade:

- 1.5 pounds (680g) beef sirloin or top sirloin, cut into 1- inch cubes
- 1/4 cup olive oil
- 3 cloves garlic, minced
- 1 tablespoon paprika
- 1 teaspoon cayenne pepper (adjust to taste)
- 1 teaspoon ground cumin
- 1 teaspoon ground coriander
- 1/2 teaspoon ground turmeric
- 1/2 teaspoon ground cinnamon
- Salt and freshly ground black pepper, to taste
- Juice of 1 lemon
- 2 tablespoons plain yogurt (optional, for tenderness) For Assembling and Grilling:
- Wooden or metal skewers (if using wooden skewers, soak them in water for 30 minutes before using)
- Bell peppers, onions, and cherry tomatoes (optional, for skewering with the beef)
- Lemon wedges, for garnish

Instructions:

1. Prepare the Marinade:

- In a bowl, combine the olive oil, minced garlic, paprika, cayenne pepper, ground cumin, ground coriander, ground turmeric, ground cinnamon, salt, black pepper, lemon juice, and optional plain yogurt.
- Mix the marinade well to create a smooth paste.

2. Marinate the Beef:

- Place the beef cubes in a large resealable plastic bag or a shallow dish.
- Pour the marinade over the beef, making sure it's well-coated.
- Seal the bag or cover the dish with plastic wrap and refrigerate for at least 2-4 hours, allowing the flavors to infuse and tenderize the meat. You can marinate it overnight for even more flavor.

3. Preheat the Grill:

- Preheat your grill to medium-high heat, around 400- 450°F (204-232°C).

4. Assemble the Kebabs:

- Thread the marinated beef cubes onto skewers, alternat- ing with bell pepper pieces, onion wedges, and cherry toma- toes if desired. This creates colorful and flavorful kebabs.

5. Grill the Kebabs:

- Place the assembled beef kebabs on the preheated grill grates.
- Grill for about 10-15 minutes, turning occasionally, until the beef reaches your preferred level of doneness. For me- dium-rare, aim for an internal temperature of 130- 135°F (54-57°C).
- Be cautious not to overcook the beef to maintain its tenderness.

6. Serve:

- Once the beef kebabs are cooked to your liking, remove them from the grill.
- Garnish with lemon wedges and additional fresh herbs if desired.
- Serve the spicy beef kebabs hot with your choice of sides, such as rice, flatbread, or a salad.

Enjoy these zesty and flavorful Spicy Beef Kebabs, perfect for grilling outdoors or at your next barbecue gathering. The combi- nation of spices and marinating time ensures a mouthwatering, tender, and spicy treat that's sure to satisfy your taste buds.

Mediterranean Spiced Beef Kebabs

Preparation Time: 30 min | Marinating Time: 2-4 hours | Cooking Time: 10-15 min
Servings: 4-6

Ingredients:
For the Beef Marinade:

- 1.5 pounds (680g) beef sirloin or ribeye, cut into 1-inch cubes
- 1/4 cup olive oil
- 3 cloves garlic, minced
- 1 teaspoon dried oregano
- 1 teaspoon dried thyme
- 1 teaspoon ground cumin
- 1/2 teaspoon smoked paprika
- 1/2 teaspoon ground coriander
- Salt and freshly ground black pepper, to taste
- Juice of 1 lemon For the Kebabs:
- 2 large tomatoes, cut into wedges
- 1 large red onion, cut into 1-inch pieces
- Wooden or metal skewers (if using wooden skewers, soak them in water for 30 minutes before using)

Instructions:
For the Beef Marinade:

1. Prepare the Marinade:

- In a bowl, combine the olive oil, minced garlic, dried oregano, dried thyme, ground cumin, smoked paprika, ground coriander, salt, black pepper, and the juice of one lemon.
- Mix well to create a flavorful Mediterranean-inspired beef marinade.

2. Marinate the Beef:

- Place the beef cubes in a large resealable plastic bag or a shallow dish.
- Pour the marinade over the beef, ensuring that it's well- coated.
- Seal the bag or cover the dish with plastic wrap and refrigerate for 2-4 hours, allowing the flavors to meld and the meat to absorb the marinade. Marinating overnight is even better if time allows.

Assembling and Grilling the Kebabs:

1. Preheat the Grill:

- Preheat your grill to medium-high heat, around 450- 500°F (232-260°C) for direct grilling.

2. Assemble the Kebabs:

- Thread the marinated beef cubes onto skewers, alternat- ing with tomato wedges and red onion pieces to create vibrant and flavorful kebabs.

3. Grill the Kebabs:

- Place the assembled Mediterranean Spiced Beef Kebabs on the preheated grill grates.
- Grill for about 3-4 minutes on each side, turning occa- sionally, until the beef is cooked to your desired level of done- ness. Aim for medium-rare to medium for the best results.

4. Check for Doneness:

- Use a meat thermometer to check the internal tempera- ture. For medium-rare, aim for an internal temperature of 130- 135°F (54-57°C).

5. Serve:

- Remove the beef kebabs from the grill and let them rest for about 5 minutes on a serving platter. This allows the juices to redistribute and ensures a juicy, tender result.

6. Serve:

- Serve the Mediterranean Spiced Beef Kebabs hot with your choice of sides, such as couscous, pita bread, or a fresh Mediterranean salad.

Enjoy the enticing flavors of these Mediterranean Spiced Beef Kebabs, combining tender beef cubes marinated in a blend of Mediterranean spices with juicy tomatoes and sweet red onions. It's a vibrant and delicious dish that captures the essence of Mediterranean cuisine and is perfect for a flavorful outdoor meal.

Classic Cheeseburger on the Grill

Preparation Time: 15 min | Cooking Time: 10-12 min
Servings: 4

Ingredients:
For the Burger Patties:

- 1.5 pounds (680g) ground beef (80% lean, 20% fat is ideal)
- Salt and freshly ground black pepper, to taste For the Toppings and Assembly:
- 4 hamburger buns
- 4 slices of your favorite cheese (American, cheddar, Swiss, etc.)
- Lettuce leaves
- Sliced tomatoes
- Sliced onions
- Pickles
- Ketchup
- Mustard
- Mayonnaise

Instructions:
Preparing the Burger Patties:

1. Preheat the Grill:

- Preheat your grill to medium-high heat, around 400- 450°F (204-232°C) for direct grilling.

2. Divide the Ground Beef:

- Divide the ground beef into 4 equal portions and shape them into burger patties, about 1/2 to 3/4 inch thick. Make sure the patties are slightly wider than the diameter of your burger buns since they will shrink during cooking. Use your thumb to create a slight indentation in the center of each patty; this helps them cook evenly and prevents them from puffing up.

3. Season the Patties:

- Season both sides of each patty generously with salt and freshly ground black pepper. You can also add your favorite seasonings or spices for extra flavor if desired.

Grilling the Burger Patties:

1. Grill the Patties:

- Place the burger patties on the preheated grill grates.
- Grill for about 4-6 minutes on each side, depending on your preferred level of doneness (rare, medium-rare, medium, or well-done). For medium-rare, aim for an internal temperature of 130-135°F (54-57°C).

2. Add Cheese (Optional):

- About 1-2 minutes before removing the patties from the grill, place a slice of cheese on each patty.
- Close the grill lid to allow the cheese to melt.

Assembling the Cheeseburgers:

1. Toast the Buns:

- While the patties are cooking, you can split the hamburger buns and lightly toast them on the grill for a minute or two, until they're golden brown.

2. Assemble the Cheeseburgers:

- Start by placing a lettuce leaf on the bottom half of each bun.
- Add a slice of tomato, a few slices of onion, and some pickles.
- Place the grilled burger patty with melted cheese on top of the veggies.
- Add condiments like ketchup, mustard, and mayonnaise according to your preference.

3. Complete the Burgers:

- Top the burger with the other half of the toasted bun.

4. Serve:

- Serve your classic cheeseburgers hot with your favorite side dishes, such as french fries, coleslaw, or a green salad.

Enjoy the simplicity and timeless deliciousness of a Classic Cheeseburger on the grill. Customize your burger with your favorite toppings and condiments to create a perfect, juicy, and flavorful meal for a barbecue or cookout.

Italian Sausage Cheese Burger with Grilled Onions

Preparation Time: 15 min | Cooking Time: 20-25 min
Servings: 4

Ingredients:
For the Burger Patties:

- 1/2 pound (225g) ground beef
- 1/2 pound (225g) ground Italian sausage (sweet or spicy, your choice)
- Salt and freshly ground black pepper, to taste
- 1 teaspoon Italian seasoning (optional) For the Grilled Onions:
- 1 large onion, thinly sliced
- 2 tablespoons olive oil
- Salt and freshly ground black pepper, to taste For Assembling the Burgers:
- 4 burger buns
- 4 slices provolone cheese
- Lettuce leaves
- Sliced tomatoes
- Ketchup and mustard (optional)

Instructions:
Preparing the Burger Patties:

1. Combine Beef and Italian Sausage:

- In a mixing bowl, combine the ground beef and ground Italian sausage.
- Season the mixture with salt, freshly ground black pepper, and Italian seasoning (if using).
- Gently mix until the meats are evenly combined.

2. Shape the Patties:

- Divide the meat mixture into 4 equal portions and shape them into burger patties, about 1/2 to 3/4 inch thick. Make sure the patties are slightly wider than the diameter of your burger buns, as they will shrink during cooking.

Grilling the Onions:

1. Preheat the Grill:

- Preheat your grill to medium-high heat, around 400- 450°F (204-232°C) for direct grilling.

2. Grill the Onions:

- In a small bowl, toss the thinly sliced onions with olive oil, salt, and freshly ground black pepper.
- Place the seasoned onions in a grill basket or on a sheet of aluminum foil on the grill grates.

- Grill the onions for about 10-15 minutes, stirring occa- sionally, until they are soft and caramelized.

Grilling the Burger Patties:

1. Grill the Patties:

- Place the burger patties on the preheated grill grates.
- Grill for about 4-6 minutes on each side, or until they reach your desired level of doneness (medium-rare, medium, or well-done).

2. Add Provolone Cheese:

- About 1-2 minutes before removing the patties from the grill, place a slice of provolone cheese on each patty.
- Close the grill lid to allow the cheese to melt.

Assembling the Burgers:

1. 1. Toast the Buns:

2. While the patties are cooking, you can split the burger buns and lightly toast them on the grill for a minute or two until they're golden brown.

3. Assemble the Burgers:

- Start by placing a lettuce leaf on the bottom half of each bun.
- Add a slice of tomato.
- Place the grilled beef and Italian sausage patty with melted provolone cheese on top.

4. Add Grilled Onions:

- Generously pile the grilled onions on top of the patty.

5. Complete the Burgers:

- Top with the other half of the toasted bun.
- Optionally, add ketchup and mustard according to your preference.

6. Serve:

- Serve your Beef and Italian Sausage Burger with Pro- volone Cheese and Grilled Onions hot with your favorite side dishes, such as french fries or coleslaw.

Enjoy this delicious and hearty burger that combines the flavors of beef and Italian sausage with the richness of melted provolone cheese and the sweetness of grilled onions. It's a savory delight that will satisfy your taste buds at your next barbecue or cookout.

Blue Cheese Burgers

Preparation Time: 15 min | Cooking Time: 10-12 min
Servings: 4

Ingredients:
For the Burger Patties:

- 1.5 pounds (680g) ground beef (80% lean, 20% fat is ideal)
- Salt and freshly ground black pepper, to taste For the Blue Cheese Mixture:
- 4 ounces (113g) crumbled blue cheese (choose your fa- vorite variety)
- 2 tablespoons mayonnaise
- 1 clove garlic, minced
- 1 tablespoon chopped fresh parsley (optional)
- Freshly ground black pepper, to taste For Assembling the Burgers:
- 4 burger buns
- Lettuce leaves
- Sliced tomatoes
- Sliced red onions
- Ketchup and mustard (optional)

Instructions:
Preparing the Burger Patties:

1. Preheat the Grill:

- Preheat your grill to medium-high heat, around 400- 450°F (204-232°C) for direct grilling.

2. Shape the Patties:

- Divide the ground beef into 4 equal portions and shape them into burger patties, about 1/2 to 3/4 inch thick. Make sure the patties are slightly wider than the diameter of your burger buns, as they will shrink during cooking.
- Season both sides of each patty generously with salt and freshly ground black pepper.

Preparing the Blue Cheese Mixture:

1. Prepare the Blue Cheese Mixture:

- In a small bowl, combine the crumbled blue cheese, mayonnaise, minced garlic, chopped fresh parsley (if using), and freshly ground black pepper.
- Mix well to create a creamy blue cheese spread.

Grilling the Burger Patties:

1. Grill the Patties:

  - Place the burger patties on the preheated grill grates.
  - Grill for about 4-6 minutes on each side, depending on your preferred level of doneness (rare, medium-rare, medium, or well-done).

2. Add Blue Cheese Mixture:

  - About 1-2 minutes before removing the patties from the grill, spread a generous amount of the blue cheese mixture on top of each patty.
  - Close the grill lid to allow the blue cheese to melt slightly.

Assembling the Burgers:

1. Toast the Buns:

  - While the patties are cooking, you can split the burger buns and lightly toast them on the grill for a minute or two, until they're golden brown.

2. Assemble the Burgers:

  - Start by placing a lettuce leaf on the bottom half of each bun.
  - Add a slice of tomato and a few slices of red onion.
  - Place the grilled blue cheese patty on top.

3. Complete the Burgers:

  - Top with the other half of the toasted bun.
  - Optionally, add ketchup and mustard according to your preference.

4. Serve:

  - Serve your Blue Cheese Burgers hot with your favorite side dishes, such as french fries, coleslaw, or a fresh green salad.

Enjoy the rich and savory flavors of these Blue Cheese Burgers, with the creamy and tangy blue cheese mixture adding a delightful twist to the classic burger. It's a perfect choice for cheeseburger enthusiasts looking for something a bit more decadent.

BBQ Burgers

Preparation Time: 20 min | Cooking Time: 10-12 min
Servings: 4

Ingredients:
For the Burger Patties:

- 1.5 pounds (680g) ground beef (80% lean, 20% fat is ideal)
- Salt and freshly ground black pepper, to taste
- 4 hamburger buns

For the Toppings:

- 4 slices cheddar cheese
- 8 strips of bacon, cooked until crispy
- 1 cup crispy onion straws or onion rings
- 1/2 cup BBQ sauce (your favorite variety)
- Lettuce leaves
- Sliced tomatoes
- Sliced red onions
- Ketchup and mustard (optional)

Instructions:

Preparing the Burger Patties:

1. Preheat the Grill:

- Preheat your grill to medium-high heat, around 400- 450°F (204-232°C) for direct grilling.

2. Shape the Patties:

- Divide the ground beef into 4 equal portions and shape them into burger patties, about 1/2 to 3/4 inch thick. Make sure the patties are slightly wider than the diameter of your burger buns, as they will shrink during cooking.
- Season both sides of each patty generously with salt and freshly ground black pepper.

Grilling the Burger Patties:

1. Grill the Patties:

- Place the burger patties on the preheated grill grates.
- Grill for about 4-6 minutes on each side, depending on your preferred level of doneness (rare, medium-rare, medium, or well-done).

2. Add Cheddar Cheese:

- About 1-2 minutes before removing the patties from the grill, place a slice of cheddar cheese on each patty.
- Close the grill lid to allow the cheese to melt.

Assembling the BBQ Burgers:

1. Toast the Buns:

- While the patties are cooking, you can split the burger buns and lightly toast them on the grill for a minute or two until they're golden brown.

2. Assemble the Burgers:

- Start by placing a lettuce leaf on the bottom half of each bun.
- Add a slice of tomato and a few slices of red onion.
- Place the grilled burger patty with melted cheddar cheese on top.

3. Add Bacon and Crispy Onion Straws:

- Lay two strips of crispy bacon on each burger.
- Pile crispy onion straws or onion rings on top of the bacon.

4. Drizzle with BBQ Sauce:

- Generously drizzle BBQ sauce over the crispy onion straws and the top half of the burger bun.

5. Complete the Burgers:

- Top with the other half of the toasted bun.
- Optionally, add ketchup and mustard according to your preference.

6. Serve:

- Serve your BBQ Burgers hot with your favorite side dishes, such as coleslaw, potato salad, or baked beans.

Enjoy the mouthwatering combination of flavors in these BBQ Burgers, with the smoky BBQ sauce, melted cheddar cheese, crispy bacon, and crunchy onion straws making each bite a delicious delight. It's the ultimate treat for burger lovers!

Grilling Recipes: Pork

Honey-Glazed Grilled Pork Chops

Preparation Time: 10 min | Marinating Time: 30 min (optional) | Cooking Time: 10-12 min
Servings: 4

Ingredients:
For the Pork Chops:

- 4 bone-in pork chops, about 1 inch thick
- Salt and freshly ground black pepper, to taste For the Honey Glaze:
- 1/4 cup honey
- 2 tablespoons soy sauce
- 2 tablespoons Dijon mustard
- 2 cloves garlic, minced
- 1 tablespoon apple cider vinegar (or white wine vinegar)
- 1 teaspoon smoked paprika (optional for added smoki- ness)
- 1/2 teaspoon ground cumin
- 1/4 teaspoon cayenne pepper (adjust to taste)
- Fresh parsley, for garnish (optional)

Instructions:
Preparing the Honey Glaze:

1. Prepare the Honey Glaze:

- · In a small bowl, whisk together the honey, soy sauce, Di- jon mustard, minced garlic, apple cider vinegar, smoked paprika (if using), ground cumin, and cayenne pepper.
- · Mix until all the ingredients are well combined. This will be your sweet and savory honey glaze.

2. Marinate the Pork Chops (optional):

- · If time allows, you can marinate the pork chops in a portion of the honey glaze for extra flavor. Place the pork chops in a resealable plastic bag and pour enough of the glaze over them to coat. Seal the bag and refrigerate for at least 30 minutes, or longer for more flavor. Reserve the remaining glaze for basting during grilling.

Grilling the Pork Chops:

1. Preheat the Grill:

- Preheat your grill to medium-high heat, around 400- 450°F (204-232°C) for direct grilling.

2. Season the Pork Chops:

- Remove the pork chops from the marinade (if marinated) and season both sides with salt and freshly ground black pepper.

3. Grill the Pork Chops:

- Place the seasoned pork chops on the preheated grill grates.
- Grill for about 4-6 minutes on each side, depending on thickness and your preferred level of doneness (pork should reach an internal temperature of 145°F or 63°C for medium-rare, or cook longer for desired doneness).
- During the last few minutes of grilling, brush the pork chops with the reserved honey glaze, turning and brush- ing them a few times to create a sticky, flavorful glaze.

4. Check for Doneness:

- Use a meat thermometer to ensure the pork chops have reached the desired internal temperature. Avoid over- cooking to keep them juicy and tender.

5. Rest and Serve:

- Remove the Honey-Glazed Grilled Pork Chops from the grill and let them rest for a few minutes before serving.
- Optionally, garnish with fresh parsley for added freshness and color.

6. Serve:

- Serve the pork chops hot with your favorite side dishes, such as roasted vegetables, rice, or a fresh garden salad.

Enjoy the succulent and sweet flavors of these Honey-Glazed Grilled Pork Chops. The honey glaze adds a delightful carame-lization to the pork chops, making them both sticky and savory. It's a perfect recipe for a delightful barbecue or outdoor dinner.

Apple Cider Brined Pork Chops

Preparation Time: 15 min | Brining Time: 4-8 hours | Cooking Time: 10-12 min
Servings: 4

Ingredients:
For the Brine:

- 4 bone-in pork chops, about 1 inch thick
- 4 cups apple cider
- 1/4 cup kosher salt
- 1/4 cup brown sugar
- 1 tablespoon whole black peppercorns
- 1 cinnamon stick
- 2 cloves garlic, minced
- 2 bay leaves
- 4 cups ice cubes For Cooking:
- 2 tablespoons olive oil
- Salt and freshly ground black pepper, to taste
- Fresh rosemary sprigs (optional, for garnish)

Instructions:
Brining the Pork Chops:

1. Prepare the Brine:

- In a large pot, combine the apple cider, kosher salt, brown sugar, whole black peppercorns, cinnamon stick, minced garlic, and bay leaves.
- Stir well to dissolve the salt and sugar. Bring the mixture to a boil over medium-high heat, then remove it from the heat.

2. Cool the Brine:

- Allow the brine to cool to room temperature. You can expedite this process by placing the pot in an ice bath.

3. Brine the Pork Chops:

- Place the pork chops in a large resealable plastic bag or a shallow dish.
- Pour the cooled brine over the pork chops, ensuring they are fully submerged.

- Add the ice cubes to the brine to help cool it down further.
- Seal the bag or cover the dish with plastic wrap and refrigerate for 4-8 hours. This allows the pork chops to absorb the flavors and become more tender.

Cooking the Pork Chops:

1. Preheat the Grill:

- Preheat your grill to medium-high heat, around 400- 450°F (204-232°C) for direct grilling.

2. Remove and Pat Dry:

- Remove the pork chops from the brine and pat them dry with paper towels.

3. Season the Pork Chops:

- Brush the pork chops with olive oil and season both sides with salt and freshly ground black pepper.

4. Grill the Pork Chops:

- Place the seasoned pork chops on the preheated grill grates.
- Grill for about 4-6 minutes on each side, depending on thickness and your preferred level of doneness (pork should reach an internal temperature of 145°F or 63°C for medium-rare, or cook longer for desired doneness).

5. Check for Doneness:

- Use a meat thermometer to ensure the pork chops have reached the desired internal temperature.

6. Rest and Serve:

- Remove the Apple Cider Brined Pork Chops from the grill and let them rest for a few minutes before serving.

7. Garnish and Serve:

- Optionally, garnish with fresh rosemary sprigs for added aroma and presentation.

Serve these Apple Cider Brined Pork Chops hot with your favorite side dishes, such as mashed potatoes, roasted veg- etables, or a crisp salad. The brining process infuses the pork chops with a subtle sweetness and depth of flavor, resulting in juicy and tender pork chops that are sure to impress.

BBQ Baby Back Ribs

Preparation Time: 15 min | Marinating Time: 2-4 hours (optional) | Cooking Time: 2.5-3 hours
Servings: 4

Ingredients:
For the Ribs:

- 2 racks of baby back ribs (approximately 2-3 pounds each)
- Salt and freshly ground black pepper, to taste For the Dry Rub:
- 1/4 cup brown sugar
- 2 tablespoons paprika
- 1 tablespoon salt
- 1 tablespoon garlic powder
- 1 tablespoon onion powder
- 1 teaspoon black pepper
- 1 teaspoon cayenne pepper (adjust to taste) For the BBQ Sauce:
- 1 1/2 cups barbecue sauce (your favorite variety)
- 1/4 cup apple cider vinegar
- 1/4 cup honey
- 2 cloves garlic, minced
- 1 tablespoon Worcestershire sauce For Smoking:
- Wood chips (hickory, apple, cherry, or your choice)

Instructions:
Preparing the Ribs:

1. Remove Membrane (optional):

- On the backside of the ribs, locate the thin membrane covering the bones.
- Using a butter knife or your fingers, loosen a corner of the membrane.
- Grab the membrane with a paper towel and pull it off in one piece. This step is optional but can make the ribs more tender.

2. Season the Ribs:

- Season both sides of the racks of baby back ribs with salt and freshly ground black pepper.

Preparing the Dry Rub:

1. Prepare the Dry Rub:

- In a bowl, combine the brown sugar, paprika, salt, garlic powder, onion powder, black pepper, and cayenne pepper.
- Mix well to create a flavorful dry rub.

2. Apply the Dry Rub:

- Generously coat both sides of the ribs with the dry rub mixture, pressing it into the meat.
- Wrap the seasoned ribs in plastic wrap and refrigerate for 2-4 hours, or overnight if possible. This allows the flavors to penetrate the meat.

Preparing the BBQ Sauce:

1. Prepare the BBQ Sauce:

- In a saucepan, combine the barbecue sauce, apple cider vinegar, honey, minced garlic, and Worcestershire sauce.
- Heat the mixture over low heat, stirring occasionally, until it's well combined and heated through.
- Remove from heat.

Smoking the Ribs:

1. Prepare the Grill for Smoking:

- Preheat your grill for indirect grilling. If using charcoal, place the lit charcoal on one side of the grill and leave the other side empty. If using a gas grill, light one burner and leave the others off.
- Soak the wood chips in water for about 30 minutes, then drain them.

2. Add Wood Chips for Smoke:

- Place the soaked wood chips in either a smoker box or in an aluminum foil pouch and place directly over the lit charcoal or on the burner cover for gas grills.
- Place a drip pan underneath the grates on the side without direct heat. This will catch drippings and prevent flare-ups.

3. Smoke the Ribs:

- Place the seasoned and refrigerated ribs on the grill grates over the drip pan (indirect heat).
- Close the grill lid and maintain a temperature of around 225-250°F (107-121°C). Add more wood chips as needed to maintain a light smoke.
- Smoke the ribs for 2.5-3 hours, or until they reach your desired level of tenderness. They should have a nice smoky flavor and be tender but not falling off the bone.

Finishing with BBQ Sauce:

1. Apply the BBQ Sauce:

- During the last 30 minutes of smoking, baste the ribs with the prepared BBQ sauce on both sides, using a brush.
- Continue to cook until the sauce is caramelized and the ribs have reached your desired level of doneness.

2. Rest and Serve:

- Remove the BBQ Baby Back Ribs from the grill and let them rest for a few minutes before serving.
- Optionally, cut the ribs into individual portions and serve with extra BBQ sauce on the side.

Enjoy these BBQ Baby Back Ribs that are slow-cooked, smoked, and glazed with a rich BBQ sauce, delivering a classic, finger-licking experience that's perfect for any barbecue or outdoor gathering.

St. Louis Style Grilled Ribs

Preparation Time: 15 min | Marinating Time: 2-4 hours (optional) | Cooking Time: 2.5-3 hours
Servings: 4

Ingredients:
For the Ribs:

- 2 racks of St. Louis-style ribs (approximately 2-3 pounds each)
- Salt and freshly ground black pepper, to taste For the Dry Rub:
- 1/4 cup brown sugar
- 2 tablespoons paprika
- 1 tablespoon salt
- 1 tablespoon garlic powder
- 1 tablespoon onion powder
- 1 teaspoon black pepper
- 1 teaspoon cayenne pepper (adjust to taste) For the Glaze:
- 1/2 cup barbecue sauce (your favorite variety)
- 2 tablespoons apple cider vinegar
- 2 tablespoons honey
- 1 teaspoon Worcestershire sauce

Instructions:
Preparing the Ribs:

1. Remove Membrane (optional):

- On the backside of the St. Louis-style ribs, locate the thin membrane covering the bones.
- Using a butter knife or your fingers, loosen a corner of the membrane.
- Grab the membrane with a paper towel and pull it off in one piece. This step is optional but can make the ribs more tender.

2. Season the Ribs:

- Season both sides of the racks of St. Louis Style ribs with salt and freshly ground black pepper.

Preparing the Dry Rub:

1. Prepare the Dry Rub:

- In a bowl, combine the brown sugar, paprika, salt, garlic powder, onion powder, black pepper, and cayenne pepper.
- Mix well to create a flavorful dry rub.

2. Apply the Dry Rub:

- Generously coat both sides of the ribs with the dry rub mixture, pressing it into the meat.
- Wrap the seasoned ribs in plastic wrap and refrigerate for 2-4 hours, or overnight if possible. This allows the flavors to penetrate the meat.

Preparing the Glaze:

1. Prepare the Glaze:

- In a saucepan, combine the barbecue sauce, apple cider vinegar, honey, and Worcestershire sauce.
- Heat the mixture over low heat, stirring occasionally, until it's well combined and heated through.
- Remove from heat.

Grilling the Ribs:

1. Preheat the Grill:

- Preheat your grill to medium-low heat, around 275-300°F (135-149°C) for indirect grilling.

2. Smoke the Ribs:

- Place the seasoned and refrigerated ribs on the grill grates away from direct heat (indirect grilling).

3. Maintain Temperature:

- Close the grill lid and maintain the temperature at around 275-300°F (135-149°C). Use the grill's vents to control the airflow and maintain consistent heat.

4. Smoke the Ribs for 2.5-3 Hours:

- Smoke the ribs for 2.5-3 hours, occasionally checking and adjusting the temperature if needed.

5. Glaze the Ribs:

- During the last 30 minutes of smoking, brush the racks of ribs with the prepared glaze on both sides, using a brush.
- Continue to cook until the glaze is caramelized, and the ribs have reached your desired level of tenderness.

6. Rest and Serve:

- Remove the St. Louis Style Grilled Ribs from the grill and let them rest for a few minutes before serving.

7. Slice and Serve:

- Optionally, slice the ribs between the bones to create individual portions.
- Serve with extra glaze on the side.

Enjoy these St. Louis Style Grilled Ribs that are seasoned with a flavorful dry rub and finished with a sweet and tangy glaze over the grill. They're perfect for a BBQ or outdoor gathering, and the distinct cut of these ribs makes them a true barbecue delight!

Garlic and Herb Marinated Pork Tenderloin

Preparation Time: 15 min | Marinating Time: 2-4 hours | Cooking Time: 20-25 min
Servings: 4

Ingredients:
For the Marinade:

- 2 pork tenderloins (about 1.5 pounds each)
- 4 cloves garlic, minced
- 2 tablespoons fresh rosemary, chopped (or 1 tablespoon dried)
- 2 tablespoons fresh thyme, chopped (or 1 tablespoon dried)
- 1/4 cup olive oil
- 2 tablespoons Dijon mustard
- 1 tablespoon honey
- 1 lemon, juiced
- Salt and freshly ground black pepper, to taste

Instructions:
Preparing the Marinade:

1. Prepare the Marinade:

- In a bowl, combine the minced garlic, chopped rosemary, chopped thyme, olive oil, Dijon mustard, honey, lemon juice, salt, and freshly ground black pepper.
- Mix well to create a flavorful marinade.

2. Marinate the Pork Tenderloins:

- Place the pork tenderloins in a large resealable plastic bag or a shallow dish.
- Pour the marinade over the pork tenderloins, ensuring they are fully coated.
- Seal the bag or cover the dish with plastic wrap and refrigerate for 2-4 hours, or overnight if possible. This allows the pork to absorb the flavors and become more tender.

Grilling the Pork Tenderloins:

1. Preheat the Grill:

- Preheat your grill to medium-high heat, around 400- 450°F (204-232°C) for direct grilling.

2. Remove the Pork from the Marinade:

- Remove the pork tenderloins from the marinade and let any excess marinade drip off.

3. Grill the Pork Tenderloins:

- Place the pork tenderloins on the preheated grill grates.
- Grill for about 20-25 minutes, turning occasionally, until the internal temperature of the pork reaches 145°F (63°C). Use a meat thermometer to ensure doneness.

4. Baste with Marinade (Optional):

- You can baste the pork tenderloins with any remaining marinade during the grilling process for added flavor.

5. Check for Doneness:

- Use a meat thermometer to ensure the pork has reached the desired internal temperature.

6. Rest and Serve:

- Remove the Garlic and Herb Marinated Pork Tenderloin from the grill and let it rest for a few minutes before slicing.

7. Slice and Serve:

- Slice the pork tenderloin into medallions and serve hot.

Enjoy this tender and flavorful Garlic and Herb Marinated Pork Tenderloin, which is grilled to perfection and infused with the rich aroma of garlic and fresh herbs. It makes for an impressive and delicious main course for any meal!

Grilled Pork Tenderloin with Peach Salsa

Preparation Time: 15 min | Marinating Time: 2-4 hours (optional) | Cooking Time: 20-25 min
Servings: 4

Ingredients:
For the Pork Tenderloin:

- 2 pork tenderloins (about 1.5 pounds each)
- 2 cloves garlic, minced
- 1 teaspoon fresh rosemary, chopped (or 1/2 teaspoon dried)
- 1 teaspoon fresh thyme, chopped (or 1/2 teaspoon dried)
- 2 tablespoons olive oil
- Salt and freshly ground black pepper, to taste For the Peach Salsa:
- 4 ripe peaches, peeled, pitted, and diced
- 1/2 red onion, finely chopped
- 1/4 cup fresh cilantro, chopped
- 1 jalapeño pepper, seeded and finely minced (adjust to taste)
- Juice of 1 lime
- Salt and freshly ground black pepper, to taste

Instructions:
Preparing the Pork Tenderloin:

1. Prepare the Marinade (Optional):

- In a bowl, combine the minced garlic, chopped rosemary, chopped thyme, olive oil, salt, and freshly ground black pepper.
- Mix well to create a simple marinade.

2. Marinate the Pork Tenderloins (Optional):

- Place the pork tenderloins in a large resealable plastic bag or a shallow dish.
- Pour the marinade over the pork tenderloins, ensuring they are fully coated.
- Seal the bag or cover the dish with plastic wrap and refrigerate for 2-4 hours, or overnight if possible. This step is optional but can enhance the flavor of the pork.

Grilling the Pork Tenderloin:

1. 1. Preheat the Grill:

    - Preheat your grill to medium-high heat, around 400- 450°F (204-232°C) for direct grilling.

2. Remove the Pork from the Marinade (if marinated):

    - Remove the pork tenderloins from the marinade and let any excess marinade drip off.

3. Grill the Pork Tenderloins:

    - Place the pork tenderloins on the preheated grill grates.
    - Grill for about 20-25 minutes, turning occasionally, until the internal temperature of the pork reaches 145°F (63°C). Use a meat thermometer to ensure doneness.

4. Check for Doneness:

    - Use a meat thermometer to ensure the pork has reached the desired internal temperature.

5. Rest and Slice:

    - Remove the Grilled Pork Tenderloin from the grill and let it rest for a few minutes before slicing.

Preparing the Peach Salsa:

1. Prepare the Peach Salsa:

    - In a bowl, combine the diced peaches, finely chopped red onion, chopped cilantro, minced jalapeño pepper, lime juice, salt, and freshly ground black pepper.
    - Mix gently to combine all the ingredients.

Serving:

1. Slice and Serve:

    - Slice the grilled pork tenderloin into medallions.
    - Serve the sliced pork tenderloin topped with the fresh peach salsa.

Enjoy this light and refreshing summer dish of Grilled Pork Tenderloin with Peach Salsa. The combination of tender grilled pork and the sweet and tangy peach salsa creates a delightful and vibrant flavor that's perfect for warm-weather meals.

Caribbean Jerk Pork Skewers

Preparation Time: 15 min | Marinating Time: 2-4 hours | Cooking Time: 10-12 min
Servings: 4

Ingredients:
For the Jerk Marinade:

- 2 pounds pork loin or pork shoulder, cut into 1-inch cubes
- 2 tablespoons olive oil
- 2 tablespoons dark rum (optional)
- 3 tablespoons soy sauce
- 3 cloves garlic, minced
- 2-3 tablespoons jerk seasoning (adjust to taste)
- 1 tablespoon brown sugar
- 1 teaspoon dried thyme (or 1 tablespoon fresh thyme leaves)
- 1 teaspoon ground allspice
- 1/2 teaspoon ground cinnamon
- 1/2 teaspoon ground nutmeg
- 1/2 teaspoon ground cloves
- 1/2 teaspoon cayenne pepper (adjust to taste)
- Salt and freshly ground black pepper, to taste For Assembling the Skewers:
- Pineapple chunks, fresh or canned
- Bell peppers, assorted colors, cut into chunks
- Wooden skewers, soaked in water for 30 minutes to prevent burning

Instructions:
Preparing the Jerk Marinade:

1. Prepare the Jerk Marinade:

- In a bowl, combine the olive oil, dark rum (if using), soy sauce, minced garlic, jerk seasoning, brown sugar, dried thyme (or fresh thyme leaves), ground allspice, ground cinnamon, ground nutmeg, ground cloves, cayenne pep- per, salt, and freshly ground black pepper.
- Mix well to create the spicy and sweet jerk marinade.

155

2. Marinate the Pork Cubes:

- Place the pork cubes in a large resealable plastic bag or a shallow dish.
- Pour the jerk marinade over the pork cubes, ensuring they are fully coated.
- Seal the bag or cover the dish with plastic wrap and refrigerate for 2-4 hours, or overnight if possible. This allows the pork to absorb the flavors.

Assembling and Grilling the Skewers:

1. Preheat the Grill:

- Preheat your grill to medium-high heat, around 400- 450°F (204-232°C) for direct grilling.

2. Assemble the Skewers:

- Thread the marinated pork cubes onto the wooden skew- ers, alternating with chunks of pineapple and bell pep- pers.
- Leave a little space between each ingredient for even cooking.

3. Grill the Skewers:

- Place the assembled skewers on the preheated grill grates.

4. Grill for 10-12 Minutes:

- Grill the skewers for about 10-12 minutes, turning occa- sionally, until the pork is cooked through and has a nice char on the outside.

5. Check for Doneness:

- Ensure that the pork reaches an internal temperature of 145°F (63°C).

6. Serve Hot:

- Remove the Caribbean Jerk Pork Skewers from the grill and let them rest for a minute or two before serving.

7. Serve with Sides:

- Serve the skewers hot with your choice of sides, such as rice, coleslaw, or a fresh salad.

Enjoy these Caribbean Jerk Pork Skewers featuring tender and flavorful pork marinated in a spicy and sweet jerk seasoning, grilled to perfection alongside pineapple and bell peppers. It's a taste of the Caribbean right from your grill!

Lemon and Rosemary Pork Kebabs

Preparation Time: 20 min | Marinating Time: 1-2 hours | Cooking Time: 10-12 min
Servings: 4

Ingredients:
For the Marinade:

- 1 1/2 pounds boneless pork loin, cut into 1-inch cubes
- Zest and juice of 2 lemons
- 3 cloves garlic, minced
- 2 tablespoons fresh rosemary, chopped (or 1 tablespoon dried)
- 1/4 cup olive oil
- Salt and freshly ground black pepper, to taste For the Kebabs:
- Wooden skewers, soaked in water for 30 minutes to prevent burning
- Red onion, cut into chunks
- Bell peppers, assorted colors, cut into chunks
- Lemon slices (optional, for garnish)
- Fresh rosemary sprigs (for garnish)

Instructions:
Preparing the Marinade:

1. Prepare the Marinade:

- In a bowl, combine the lemon zest, lemon juice, minced garlic, chopped rosemary, olive oil, salt, and freshly ground black pepper.
- Mix well to create a zesty and aromatic marinade.

2. Marinate the Pork Cubes:

- Place the pork cubes in a large resealable plastic bag or a shallow dish.
- Pour the lemon and rosemary marinade over the pork cubes, ensuring they are fully coated.
- Seal the bag or cover the dish with plastic wrap and refrigerate for 1-2 hours. This allows the pork to absorb the flavors.

Assembling and Grilling the Kebabs:

1. 1. Preheat the Grill:

   · Preheat your grill to medium-high heat, around 400- 450°F (204-232°C) for direct grilling.

2. Assemble the Kebabs:

   · Thread the marinated pork cubes onto the wooden skew- ers, alternating with chunks of red onion and bell peppers.
   · Leave a little space between each ingredient for even cooking.

3. Grill the Kebabs:

   · Place the assembled kebabs on the preheated grill grates.

4. Grill for 10-12 Minutes:

   · Grill the kebabs for about 10-12 minutes, turning occasionally, until the pork is cooked through and has a nice char on the outside.

5. Check for Doneness:

   · Ensure that the pork reaches an internal temperature of 145°F (63°C).

6. Serve Hot:

   · Remove the Lemon and Rosemary Pork Kebabs from the grill and let them rest for a minute or two before serving.

7. Garnish and Serve:

   · Garnish with lemon slices and fresh rosemary sprigs, if desired.

Enjoy these Lemon and Rosemary Pork Kebabs that feature zesty and aromatic flavors with a Mediterranean twist. The combination of lemon and rosemary adds brightness and depth to the tender grilled pork, making it a delightful and refreshing dish for any occasion.

Grilling Recipes: Poultry

Lemon-Brined Grilled Chicken Breasts

Preparation Time: 15 min | Brining Time: 2-4 hours | Cooking Time: 12-15 min
Servings: 4

Ingredients:
For the Brine:

- 4 boneless, skinless chicken breasts
- 4 cups cold water
- Zest and juice of 2 lemons
- 1/4 cup kosher salt
- 1/4 cup granulated sugar
- 4-6 garlic cloves, smashed
- 2-3 sprigs fresh rosemary or thyme (optional)
- 1 bay leaf For Grilling:
- Olive oil for brushing
- Salt and freshly ground black pepper, to taste
- Lemon wedges and fresh herbs for garnish (optional)

Instructions:
Preparing the Brine:

1. Create the Brine:

- In a large bowl, combine the cold water, lemon zest, lemon juice, kosher salt, granulated sugar, smashed garlic cloves, fresh rosemary or thyme (if using), and a bay leaf.
- Stir well to dissolve the salt and sugar, creating a lemony brine.

2. Submerge the Chicken:

- Place the boneless, skinless chicken breasts into a reseal- able plastic bag or a shallow dish.
- Pour the lemon brine over the chicken to completely submerge it.

3. Brine the Chicken:

- Seal the bag or cover the dish with plastic wrap and refrigerate for 2-4 hours. Brining allows the chicken to become tender, moist, and flavorful.

Grilling the Chicken Breasts:

1. Preheat the Grill:

- Preheat your grill to medium-high heat, around 400- 450°F (204-232°C) for direct grilling.

2. Remove Chicken from Brine:

- Remove the chicken breasts from the brine and pat them dry with paper towels.

3. Brush with Olive Oil:

- Brush the chicken breasts lightly with olive oil on both sides.

4. Season with Salt and Pepper:

- Season the chicken breasts with salt and freshly ground black pepper to taste.

5. Grill the Chicken:

- Place the chicken breasts on the preheated grill grates.
- Grill for approximately 6-7 minutes per side, or until the internal temperature reaches 165°F (74°C) and the chicken is no longer pink in the center.

6. Check for Doneness:

- Use a meat thermometer to ensure the chicken has reached the desired internal temperature.

7. Rest and Serve:

- Remove the Lemon-Brined Grilled Chicken Breasts from the grill and let them rest for a few minutes before serving.

8. Garnish and Serve:

- Garnish with lemon wedges and fresh herbs, if desired.

Enjoy these Lemon-Brined Grilled Chicken Breasts, which are tender, juicy, and packed with zesty flavor. The brining process infuses the chicken with a delightful lemony essence, making it a perfect dish for a summer barbecue or any outdoor gathering.

Smoky BBQ Chicken Wings

Preparation Time: 15 min | Marinating Time: 1-2 hours (optional) | Cooking Time: 20-25 min
Servings: 4

Ingredients:
For the Chicken Wings:

- 2 pounds chicken wings, split into drumettes and flats
- 2 tablespoons olive oil
- Salt and freshly ground black pepper, to taste For the Smoky BBQ Sauce:
- 1 cup ketchup
- 1/4 cup brown sugar
- 1/4 cup apple cider vinegar
- 2 tablespoons molasses
- 2 tablespoons Worcestershire sauce
- 2 teaspoons smoked paprika
- 1 teaspoon garlic powder
- 1 teaspoon onion powder
- 1/2 teaspoon cayenne pepper (adjust to taste)
- Salt and freshly ground black pepper, to taste

Instructions:
Preparing the Smoky BBQ Sauce:

1. Prepare the BBQ Sauce:

- In a saucepan over medium heat, combine the ketchup, brown sugar, apple cider vinegar, molasses, Worces-tershire sauce, smoked paprika, garlic powder, onion powder, cayenne pepper, salt, and freshly ground black pepper.
- Stir well to combine all the ingredients.

2. Simmer and Reduce:

- Bring the mixture to a boil, then reduce the heat to low.
- Simmer for 10-15 minutes, stirring occasionally, until the sauce thickens and develops a rich, smoky flavor.
- Remove the saucepan from heat and set the BBQ sauce aside.

Preparing the Chicken Wings:

1. Marinate the Chicken (Optional):

- In a large bowl, combine the chicken wings, olive oil, salt, and freshly ground black pepper.
- Toss to coat the wings evenly.
- If time allows, you can marinate the chicken in the refrigerator for 1-2 hours, but it's optional.

2. Preheat the Grill:

- Preheat your grill to medium-high heat, around 400- 450°F (204-232°C) for direct grilling.

3. Grill the Chicken Wings:

- Place the marinated chicken wings on the preheated grill grates.

4. Grill for 20-25 Minutes:

- Grill the chicken wings for about 20-25 minutes, turning occasionally, until they are crispy, fully cooked, and have a nice char.
- Baste the wings with the smoky BBQ sauce during the last 5-10 minutes of grilling, turning and basting to create a delicious glaze.

5. Check for Doneness:

- Ensure that the chicken wings have reached an internal temperature of 165°F (74°C) and are no longer pink inside.

6. Serve Hot:

- Remove the Smoky BBQ Chicken Wings from the grill.

7. Serve with Extra Sauce:

- Serve the grilled chicken wings hot, accompanied by extra smoky BBQ sauce for dipping.

Enjoy these Smoky BBQ Chicken Wings that are coated in a homemade smoky BBQ sauce and grilled to perfection. They're ideal for game day, barbecues, or any gathering where you want to savor the savory and smoky flavors of perfectly grilled wings.

Honey Mustard Grilled Chicken Wings

Preparation Time: 15 min | Marinating Time: 1-2 hours (optional) | Cooking Time: 20-25 min
Servings: 4

Ingredients:
For the Honey Mustard Marinade:

- 2 pounds chicken wings, split into drumettes and flats
- 1/2 cup Dijon mustard
- 1/4 cup honey
- 2 tablespoons olive oil
- 2 tablespoons lemon juice
- 2 cloves garlic, minced
- 1 teaspoon paprika
- Salt and freshly ground black pepper, to taste For Grilling:
- Olive oil for brushing
- Chopped fresh parsley (for garnish, optional)

Instructions:
Preparing the Honey Mustard Marinade:

1. Create the Marinade:

- In a bowl, combine the Dijon mustard, honey, olive oil, lemon juice, minced garlic, paprika, salt, and freshly ground black pepper.
- Whisk the ingredients together until you have a smooth and sweet honey mustard marinade.

2. Marinate the Chicken:

- Place the chicken wings in a large resealable plastic bag or a shallow dish.
- Pour the honey mustard marinade over the chicken wings, ensuring that all pieces are well coated.
- Seal the bag or cover the dish with plastic wrap and refrigerate for 1-2 hours if time allows, to enhance the flavor. You can skip marinating if you're short on time.

Grilling the Honey Mustard Chicken Wings:

1. Preheat the Grill:

   · Preheat your grill to medium-high heat, around 375- 400°F (190-204°C) for direct grilling.

2. Remove Chicken from Marinade:

   · Remove the chicken wings from the marinade, allowing any excess to drip off.

3. Brush with Olive Oil:

   · Brush each chicken wing lightly with olive oil to prevent sticking and promote a crispy exterior.

4. Grill the Chicken:

   · Place the chicken wings on the preheated grill grates.

5. Grill for 20-25 Minutes:

   · Grill the wings for about 20-25 minutes, turning occa- sionally, until they are cooked through and have a golden brown, slightly caramelized exterior.

6. Check for Doneness:

   · Ensure that the chicken wings reach an internal tempera- ture of 165°F (74°C).

7. Serve Hot:

   · Remove the Honey Mustard Grilled Chicken Wings from the grill.

8. Garnish and Serve:

   · Garnish with chopped fresh parsley, if desired.

Enjoy these Honey Mustard Grilled Chicken Wings, which are coated in a sweet and tangy honey mustard sauce and grilled to perfection. They make a fantastic appetizer or main dish for any occasion, and the combination of flavors is sure to be a crowd-pleaser!

Beer Can Grilled Chicken

Preparation Time: 15 min | Cooking Time: 1.5-2 hours
Servings: 4

Ingredients:

- 1 whole chicken (approximately 4-5 pounds)
- 1 can of beer (12 ounces)
- 2 tablespoons olive oil
- 2 tablespoons paprika
- 2 teaspoons garlic powder
- 2 teaspoons onion powder
- 2 teaspoons dried thyme
- 2 teaspoons dried rosemary
- 1 teaspoon salt
- 1 teaspoon freshly ground black pepper
- 1 lemon, cut in half
- Fresh herbs (rosemary, thyme, or parsley) for garnish (optional)

Instructions:

1. Preheat the Grill:

- Preheat your grill to medium-high heat, around 350- 375°F (177-190°C) for indirect grilling.

2. Prepare the Chicken:

- Remove any giblets from the chicken cavity and pat it dry with paper towels.
- Rub the chicken with olive oil, ensuring it's coated evenly.

3. Prepare the Rub:

- In a small bowl, mix together the paprika, garlic powder, onion powder, dried thyme, dried rosemary, salt, and freshly ground black pepper to create a flavorful rub.

4. Season the Chicken:

- Sprinkle the rub mixture evenly over the entire surface of the chicken, both outside and inside the cavity. Use your fingers to massage the rub into the skin.

5. Open the Beer Can:

- Open the can of beer and take several sips or pour out a small amount to make space for the chicken.

6. Insert the Beer Can:

- Place the opened beer can on a flat surface.
- Carefully slide the chicken cavity over the beer can so that the chicken is sitting upright with the can inserted into the cavity. The chicken should stand on the can and grill vertically.

7. Add Lemon Halves:

- Place the halved lemon over the neck cavity of the chicken, stabilizing it further and adding extra flavor.

8. Grill the Chicken:

- Carefully place the chicken, standing on the beer can, onto the grill grates, in the area with indirect heat.
- Close the grill lid and cook for 1.5-2 hours, or until the chicken's internal temperature reaches 165°F (74°C) and the skin is golden and crispy.

9. Remove from Grill:

- Carefully remove the Beer Can Grilled Chicken from the grill by gently gripping the beer can and using tongs or oven mitts.
- Let the chicken rest for a few minutes before carefully removing the beer can.

10. Carve and Serve:

- Carve the chicken into serving portions.
- Garnish with fresh herbs, if desired.

Enjoy your Beer Can Grilled Chicken, infused with moisture and flavor from the beer as it cooks, resulting in a juicy and flavorful bird with crispy skin. It's a fun and delicious way to grill a whole chicken!

Spicy Grilled Jerk Chicken

Preparation Time: 20 min | Marinating Time: 2-4 hours (or overnight) | Cooking Time: 20-25 min
Servings: 4

Ingredients:
For the Jerk Marinade:

- 8 chicken pieces (thighs, drumsticks, or a combination)
- 4-6 Scotch bonnet peppers (adjust to taste, remove seeds for less heat)
- 4 cloves garlic, peeled
- 1 small onion, roughly chopped
- 2 green onions (spring onions), chopped
- 2 tablespoons fresh thyme leaves (or 1 tablespoon dried)
- 1 tablespoon ground allspice
- 1 tablespoon ground cinnamon
- 1 tablespoon ground nutmeg
- 2 tablespoons soy sauce
- 2 tablespoons vegetable oil
- Juice of 2 limes
- Salt and freshly ground black pepper, to taste For Grilling:
- Olive oil for brushing
- Lime wedges for garnish (optional)

Instructions:
Preparing the Jerk Marinade:

1. Create the Jerk Marinade:

- In a blender or food processor, combine the Scotch bonnet peppers, garlic cloves, chopped onion, green onions, fresh thyme leaves, ground allspice, ground cinnamon, ground nutmeg, soy sauce, vegetable oil, lime juice, salt, and freshly ground black pepper.
- Blend until you have a smooth and fiery jerk marinade.

2. Marinate the Chicken:

- Place the chicken pieces in a large resealable plastic bag or a shallow dish.

169

- Pour the jerk marinade over the chicken, ensuring all pieces are well coated.
- Seal the bag or cover the dish with plastic wrap and refrigerate for 2-4 hours, or overnight for the best flavor.

Grilling the Jerk Chicken:

1. Preheat the Grill:

- Preheat your grill to medium-high heat, around 400- 450°F (204-232°C) for direct grilling.

2. Remove Chicken from Marinade:

- Remove the chicken pieces from the marinade, allowing any excess to drip off.

3. Brush with Olive Oil:

- Brush each chicken piece lightly with olive oil to prevent sticking and help achieve a crispy exterior.

4. Grill the Chicken:

- Place the chicken pieces on the preheated grill grates.

5. Grill for 20-25 Minutes:

- Grill the chicken for about 20-25 minutes, turning occasionally, until the chicken is cooked through and has a charred, spicy exterior.

6. Check for Doneness:

- Ensure the chicken reaches an internal temperature of 165°F (74°C) and is no longer pink inside.

7. Rest and Serve:

- Remove the Spicy Grilled Jerk Chicken from the grill and let it rest for a few minutes before serving.

8. Garnish and Serve:

- Garnish with lime wedges for an extra burst of flavor (optional).

Enjoy your Spicy Grilled Jerk Chicken, packed with the fiery and aromatic flavors of traditional Jamaican jerk seasoning. Serve it with your favorite side dishes and savor the bold and spicy taste of this classic grilled chicken dish.

Asian-Inspired Sesame Ginger Chicken Skewers

Preparation Time: 20 min | Marinating Time: 1-2 hours (or overnight) | Cooking Time: 10-12 min
Servings: 4

Ingredients:
For the Sesame Ginger Marinade:

- 1 1/2 pounds boneless, skinless chicken breasts or thighs, cut into 1-inch chunks
- 1/4 cup soy sauce
- 2 tablespoons sesame oil
- 2 tablespoons rice vinegar
- 2 tablespoons honey
- 1 tablespoon fresh ginger, grated
- 2 cloves garlic, minced
- 1 tablespoon sesame seeds
- 1 green onion, finely chopped (for garnish)
- Salt and freshly ground black pepper, to taste For Skewering:
- Wooden skewers, soaked in water for 30 minutes to prevent burning
- Bell peppers, assorted colors, cut into chunks
- Red onion, cut into chunks
- Pineapple chunks (fresh or canned)

Instructions:
Preparing the Sesame Ginger Marinade:

1. Create the Marinade:

   - In a bowl, combine the soy sauce, sesame oil, rice vinegar, honey, grated fresh ginger, minced garlic, sesame seeds, salt, and freshly ground black pepper.
   - Stir well to create a sweet and tangy sesame ginger marinade.

2. Marinate the Chicken:

   - Place the chicken chunks in a large resealable plastic bag or a shallow dish.
   - Pour the sesame ginger marinade over the chicken, en- suring that all pieces are fully coated.

- Seal the bag or cover the dish with plastic wrap and refrigerate for 1-2 hours, or overnight if possible, to allow the flavors to infuse the chicken.

Assembling and Grilling the Skewers:

1. Preheat the Grill:

- Preheat your grill to medium-high heat, around 400- 450°F (204-232°C) for direct grilling.

2. Assemble the Skewers:

- Thread the marinated chicken chunks onto the wooden skewers, alternating with chunks of bell peppers, red onion, and pineapple.
- Leave a little space between each ingredient for even cooking.

3. Grill the Skewers:

- Place the assembled skewers on the preheated grill grates.

4. Grill for 10-12 Minutes:

- Grill the skewers for about 10-12 minutes, turning occa- sionally, until the chicken is cooked through, has a nice char, and is no longer pink inside.

5. Check for Doneness:

- Ensure that the chicken reaches an internal temperature of 165°F (74°C).

6. Serve Hot:

- Remove the Asian-Inspired Sesame Ginger Chicken Skew- ers from the grill.

7. Garnish and Serve:

- Garnish with finely chopped green onions and serve hot.

Enjoy these Asian-Inspired Sesame Ginger Chicken Skewers, featuring a sweet and tangy marinade that pairs perfectly with the charred, grilled chicken and colorful vegetables. It's a delightful and flavorful twist on traditional chicken skewers with an Asian flair.

Mediterranean Stuffed Chicken Breasts

Preparation Time: 20 min | Cooking Time: 20-25 min
Servings: 4

Ingredients:
For the Stuffed Chicken Breasts:

- 4 boneless, skinless chicken breasts
- 1 cup crumbled feta cheese
- 1/2 cup sun-dried tomatoes, chopped
- 1 cup fresh spinach leaves
- 2 cloves garlic, minced
- 1 tablespoon olive oil
- Salt and freshly ground black pepper, to taste
- Toothpicks or kitchen twine (to secure the stuffed chicken)

For the Mediterranean Marinade:

- 1/4 cup olive oil
- 2 tablespoons lemon juice
- 1 teaspoon dried oregano
- 1 teaspoon dried basil
- 1 teaspoon dried thyme
- 1 teaspoon paprika
- Salt and freshly ground black pepper, to taste

Instructions:
Preparing the Mediterranean Marinade:

1. Create the Marinade:

- In a bowl, combine the olive oil, lemon juice, dried oregano, dried basil, dried thyme, paprika, salt, and freshly ground black pepper.
- Stir well to create a flavorful Mediterranean marinade.

Preparing the Stuffed Chicken Breasts:

1. Butterfly the Chicken Breasts:

   - Lay each chicken breast flat on a cutting board.
   - Carefully slice horizontally through the thickest part of each chicken breast, almost all the way through, creating a pocket for the stuffing.
   - Be careful not to cut all the way through; you want to create a flap that can be folded back.

2. Season the Chicken:

   - Season the inside of each chicken breast with salt and freshly ground black pepper.

3. Prepare the Stuffing:

   - In a skillet, heat the olive oil over medium heat.
   - Add minced garlic and sauté for about 1 minute, or until fragrant.
   - Add the chopped sun-dried tomatoes and cook for another 2-3 minutes, until they start to soften.
   - Stir in the fresh spinach leaves and cook until wilted.
   - Remove the skillet from heat and let the mixture cool slightly.
   - Stir in the crumbled feta cheese.

4. Stuff the Chicken Breasts:

   - Spoon the sun-dried tomato, spinach, and feta mixture into each chicken breast's pocket.
   - Fold the chicken flap over the stuffing to enclose it.
   - Secure each stuffed chicken breast with toothpicks or kitchen twine to hold the filling inside.

Grilling the Stuffed Chicken:

1. Preheat the Grill:

   - Preheat your grill to medium-high heat, around 375- 400°F (190-204°C) for direct grilling.

2. Brush with Marinade:

- Brush the stuffed chicken breasts with the Mediterranean marinade on all sides.

3. Grill the Chicken:

- Place the stuffed chicken breasts on the preheated grill grates.

4. Grill for 20-25 Minutes:

- Grill the chicken for about 20-25 minutes, turning occa- sionally, until the chicken is cooked through and has a beautiful grill mark.

5. Check for Doneness:

- Ensure that the chicken reaches an internal temperature of 165°F (74°C).

6. Remove Toothpicks or Twine:

- Carefully remove the toothpicks or kitchen twine from the cooked stuffed chicken breasts.

7. Serve Hot:

- Serve the Mediterranean Stuffed Chicken Breasts hot, garnished with a sprinkle of fresh herbs, if desired.

Enjoy your Mediterranean Stuffed Chicken Breasts, filled with the delightful combination of feta cheese, sun-dried tomatoes, and spinach. The grilled chicken is moist, flavorful, and perfect for a Mediterranean-inspired meal.

Tandoori-Style Grilled Chicken

Preparation Time: 15 min | Marinating Time: 2-4 hours (or overnight) | Cooking Time: 25-30 min
Servings: 4

Ingredients:
For the Tandoori Marinade:

- 4 bone-in, skin-on chicken thighs and drumsticks (or whole chicken pieces)
- 1 cup plain yogurt
- 2 tablespoons tandoori masala spice blend
- 2 tablespoons lemon juice
- 2 cloves garlic, minced
- 1-inch piece of ginger, grated
- 1 teaspoon ground cumin
- 1 teaspoon ground coriander
- 1/2 teaspoon ground turmeric
- 1/2 teaspoon paprika (for color)
- 1/2 teaspoon cayenne pepper (adjust to taste)
- Salt and freshly ground black pepper, to taste For Grilling:
- Olive oil for brushing
- Lemon wedges and fresh cilantro for garnish (optional)

Instructions:
Preparing the Tandoori Marinade:

1. Create the Marinade:

- In a bowl, combine the plain yogurt, tandoori masala spice blend, lemon juice, minced garlic, grated ginger, ground cumin, ground coriander, ground turmeric, pa- prika, cayenne pepper, salt, and freshly ground black pepper.
- Mix the ingredients until you have a well-blended tan- doori marinade.

2. Marinate the Chicken:

- Place the chicken pieces in a large resealable plastic bag or a shallow dish.
- Pour the tandoori marinade over the chicken, making sure all pieces are fully coated.
- Seal the bag or cover the dish with plastic wrap and refrigerate for 2-4 hours, or overnight for the best flavor.

Grilling the Tandoori-Style Chicken:

1. Preheat the Grill:

- Preheat your grill to medium-high heat, around 375-400°F (190-204°C) for direct grilling.

2. Remove Chicken from Marinade:

- Remove the chicken pieces from the marinade, allowing any excess to drip off.

3. Brush with Olive Oil:

- Brush each chicken piece lightly with olive oil to prevent sticking and promote a crispy exterior.

4. Grill the Chicken:

- Place the chicken pieces on the preheated grill grates.

5. Grill for 25-30 Minutes:

- Grill the chicken for about 25-30 minutes, turning oc- casionally, until they are cooked through and have a beautiful char.

6. Check for Doneness:

- Ensure that the chicken reaches an internal temperature of 165°F (74°C).

7. Serve Hot:

- Remove the Tandoori-Style Grilled Chicken from the grill.

8. Garnish and Serve:

- Garnish with lemon wedges and fresh cilantro, if desired.

Enjoy your Tandoori-Style Grilled Chicken, featuring the rich and aromatic flavors of authentic Indian tandoori spices and yogurt marinade. It's a delightful and flavorful dish that's perfect for a barbecue or any special occasion.

Tex-Mex Grilled Chicken Fajitas

Preparation Time: 20 min | Marinating Time: 1-2 hours (optional) | Cooking Time: 15-20 min
Servings: 4

Ingredients:
For the Chicken Marinade:

- 1 1/2 pounds boneless, skinless chicken breasts, sliced into thin strips
- 3 tablespoons olive oil
- 2 tablespoons lime juice
- 2 cloves garlic, minced
- 1 teaspoon ground cumin
- 1 teaspoon chili powder
- 1/2 teaspoon paprika
- 1/2 teaspoon dried oregano
- Salt and freshly ground black pepper, to taste For Grilling:
- 2 bell peppers (assorted colors), thinly sliced
- 1 red onion, thinly sliced
- Olive oil for grilling
- 8 small flour tortillas
- Sour cream, guacamole, salsa, and shredded cheese (for serving, optional)
- Lime wedges for garnish (optional)

Instructions:
Preparing the Chicken Marinade:

1. Create the Marinade:

- In a bowl, combine the olive oil, lime juice, minced garlic, ground cumin, chili powder, paprika, dried oregano, salt, and freshly ground black pepper.
- Mix the ingredients well to create a flavorful Tex-Mex chicken marinade.

2. Marinate the Chicken:

- Place the sliced chicken strips in a large resealable plastic bag or a shallow dish.
- Pour the Tex-Mex chicken marinade over the chicken, ensuring all pieces are well coated. Seal the bag or cover the dish with plastic wrap and refrigerate for 1-2 hours, allowing the flavors to meld. You can skip marinating if you're short on time.

Grilling the Tex-Mex Chicken Fajitas:

1. Preheat the Grill:

   · Preheat your grill to medium-high heat, around 375- 400°F (190-204°C) for direct grilling.

2. Prepare the Vegetables:

   · Toss the thinly sliced bell peppers and red onion with a little olive oil to prevent sticking.

3. Grill the Chicken and Vegetables:

   · Place the marinated chicken strips and prepared vegeta- bles on the preheated grill grates.
   · Grill for about 15-20 minutes, turning occasionally, until the chicken is cooked through, and the vegetables are tender and slightly charred.

4. Warm the Tortillas:

   · While the chicken and vegetables are grilling, warm the flour tortillas on the grill for a minute or two, flipping them as needed until they are warm and pliable.

5. Check for Doneness:

   · Ensure that the chicken reaches an internal temperature of 165°F (74°C).

6. Assemble the Fajitas:

   · To assemble the Tex-Mex Grilled Chicken Fajitas, place some grilled chicken and vegetables in the center of each warm tortilla.

7. Add Toppings (Optional):

   · Top with sour cream, guacamole, salsa, shredded cheese, or any of your favorite fajita toppings.

8. Serve Hot:

   · Garnish with lime wedges for an extra burst of flavor, if desired.

Enjoy your Tex-Mex Grilled Chicken Fajitas, filled with per- fectly seasoned chicken and grilled vegetables, wrapped in warm tortillas. It's a delightful Tex-Mex dish that's perfect for a casual meal with family and friends.

Grilled Quesadilla Recipe

Prep Time: 10 min | Grilling Time: 5-7 min | Total Time: 15-17 min
Servings: 4

Ingredients:

- 8 medium-sized flour tortillas
- 2 cups shredded cheese (cheddar, Monterey Jack, or your choice)
- 1 cup cooked chicken, diced (optional)
- 1/2 cup diced bell peppers (any color)
- 1/2 cup diced onions
- 1/2 cup diced tomatoes
- 2 tablespoons fresh cilantro, chopped (optional)
- 1 teaspoon ground cumin (optional)
- Olive oil or cooking spray for brushing

For Serving (Optional):

- Salsa
- Guacamole
- Sour cream

Instructions:

1. Preheat the Grill:

- Preheat your grill to medium-high heat (about 350-400°F or 175-200°C).

2. Prepare the Quesadilla Filling:

- In a bowl, combine the shredded cheese, diced cooked chicken (if using), diced bell peppers, diced onions, diced tomatoes, fresh cilantro (if using), and ground cumin (if using). Mix well to create the quesadilla filling.

3. Assemble the Quesadillas:

- Lay out four tortillas on a clean surface.
- Divide the quesadilla filling equally among the tortillas, spreading it out evenly to cover one-half of each tortilla.
- Place the remaining four tortillas on top to create que- sadilla sandwiches.

4. Grill the Quesadillas:

- Brush the outside of each quesadilla with olive oil or spray with cooking spray to prevent sticking to the grill.
- Place the quesadillas directly on the preheated grill grates.
- Grill for about 2-3 minutes on each side, or until the tortillas are crispy and have grill marks, and the cheese inside has melted.

5. Serve:

- Remove the grilled quesadillas from the grill and place them on a cutting board.

6. Slice and Enjoy:

- Use a sharp knife or pizza cutter to slice each quesadilla into wedges.
- Serve your grilled quesadillas hot with salsa, guacamole, and sour cream on the side if desired.

7. Enjoy:

These grilled quesadillas are a delightful and customiz- able meal or snack. The grill adds a smoky flavor and crispy texture to the classic quesadilla, making it perfect for outdoor gatherings or a quick and delicious weeknight dinner.

Grilling Recipes: Seafood

Asian Glazed Grilled Halibut

Preparation Time: 15 min | Marinating Time: 30 min | Cooking Time: 10-12 min
Servings: 4

Ingredients:
For the Asian Glaze:

- 1/4 cup soy sauce
- 2 tablespoons honey
- 2 tablespoons rice vinegar
- 1 tablespoon fresh ginger, grated
- 2 cloves garlic, minced
- 1 teaspoon sesame oil
- 1/4 teaspoon red pepper flakes (adjust to taste)
- 2 tablespoons chopped green onions (for garnish, op- tional)

For the Halibut:

- 4 halibut fillets (6-8 ounces each)
- Olive oil for brushing
- Salt and freshly ground black pepper, to taste
- Lemon wedges (for garnish, optional)

Instructions:
Preparing the Asian Glaze:

1. Create the Glaze:

- In a bowl, combine the soy sauce, honey, rice vinegar, grated fresh ginger, minced garlic, sesame oil, and red pepper flakes.
- Mix the ingredients until you have a sweet and savory Asian glaze.

2. Marinate the Halibut:

- Place the halibut fillets in a shallow dish or a resealable plastic bag.
- Pour half of the Asian glaze over the halibut fillets, reserv- ing the other half for later.
- Ensure the halibut is well coated in the marinade.

- Cover the dish or seal the bag and refrigerate for 30 minutes, allowing the flavors to infuse the fish. You can marinate longer for even more flavor.

Grilling the Asian Glazed Halibut:

1. Preheat the Grill:

- Preheat your grill to medium-high heat, around 375- 400°F (190-204°C) for direct grilling.

2. Remove Halibut from Marinade:

- Remove the halibut fillets from the marinade, allowing any excess marinade to drip off.

3. Brush with Olive Oil:

- Brush each side of the halibut fillets lightly with olive oil to prevent sticking and promote a nice sear.

4. Season with Salt and Pepper:

- Season the halibut fillets with salt and freshly ground black pepper to taste.

5. Grill the Halibut:

- Place the halibut fillets on the preheated grill grates.

6. Grill for 5-6 Minutes per Side:

- Grill the halibut for about 5-6 minutes per side, or until the fish is opaque and flakes easily with a fork.

7. Brush with Reserved Glaze:

- During the last few minutes of grilling, brush the re- served Asian glaze onto the halibut fillets, allowing it to caramelize slightly.

8. Garnish and Serve:

- Remove the Asian Glazed Grilled Halibut from the grill.
- Garnish with chopped green onions and lemon wedges if desired.

Enjoy your Asian Glazed Grilled Halibut, featuring tender and flaky halibut fillets infused with the sweet and savory flavors of the Asian glaze. This dish offers a perfect balance of flavors that will impress your taste buds and make for a memorable meal.

Grilled Lemon Garlic Salmon

Preparation Time: 15 min | Marinating Time: 30 min | Cooking Time: 10-12 min
Servings: 4

Ingredients:
For the Lemon Garlic Marinade:

- 4 salmon fillets (6-8 ounces each)
- 1/4 cup fresh lemon juice
- 2 cloves garlic, minced
- 2 tablespoons olive oil
- 1 teaspoon fresh thyme leaves (or 1/2 teaspoon dried)
- 1 teaspoon fresh rosemary leaves (or 1/2 teaspoon dried)
- Salt and freshly ground black pepper, to taste
- Lemon wedges and fresh parsley (for garnish, optional)

Instructions:
Preparing the Lemon Garlic Marinade:

1. Create the Marinade:

- In a bowl, combine the fresh lemon juice, minced garlic, olive oil, fresh thyme leaves, fresh rosemary leaves, salt, and freshly ground black pepper.
- Stir the ingredients together to create a fragrant lemon garlic marinade.

2. Marinate the Salmon:

- Place the salmon fillets in a shallow dish or a resealable plastic bag.
- Pour the lemon garlic marinade over the salmon, ensuring each fillet is well coated.
- Cover the dish or seal the bag and refrigerate for 30 minutes to allow the flavors to meld. You can marinate longer for even more flavor.

Grilling the Lemon Garlic Salmon:

1. Preheat the Grill:

- Preheat your grill to medium-high heat, around 375-400°F (190-204°C) for direct grilling.

2. Remove Salmon from Marinade:

- Remove the salmon fillets from the marinade, allowing any excess marinade to drip off.

3. Brush with Olive Oil:

- Brush each side of the salmon fillets lightly with olive oil to prevent sticking and promote a nice sear.

4. Season with Salt and Pepper:

- Season the salmon fillets with a pinch of salt and freshly ground black pepper to taste.

5. Grill the Salmon:

- Place the salmon fillets on the preheated grill grates.

6. Grill for 5-6 Minutes per Side:

- Grill the salmon for about 5-6 minutes per side, or until the fish is opaque and flakes easily with a fork.

7. Check for Doneness:

- Ensure the salmon reaches an internal temperature of 145°F (63°C).

8. Garnish and Serve:

- Remove the Grilled Lemon Garlic Salmon from the grill.
- Garnish with lemon wedges and fresh parsley, if desired.

Enjoy your Grilled Lemon Garlic Salmon, featuring tender and flaky salmon fillets infused with the bright and zesty flavors of lemon and garlic. It's a simple yet incredibly flavorful dish that's perfect for a healthy and delicious meal.

Cedar Plank Grilled Trout

Preparation Time: 15 min | Marinating Time: 30 min (optional) | Cooking Time: 20-25 min
Servings: 2-4

Ingredients:
For the Cedar Plank:

- 1 untreated cedar plank (sized to fit your trout)
- Water for soaking the cedar plank For the Trout and Marinade:
- 2 whole trout, gutted and cleaned
- 1/4 cup olive oil
- 2 cloves garlic, minced
- 2 tablespoons fresh lemon juice
- 1 teaspoon lemon zest
- 1 teaspoon fresh thyme leaves (or 1/2 teaspoon dried)
- 1 teaspoon fresh rosemary leaves (or 1/2 teaspoon dried)
- Salt and freshly ground black pepper, to taste
- Lemon slices and fresh herbs (for garnish, optional)

Instructions:
Preparing the Cedar Plank:

1. Soak the Cedar Plank:

- Place the untreated cedar plank in a large container or sink.
- Cover it completely with water and let it soak for at least 1-2 hours, or preferably overnight.
- Ensure the plank is fully submerged during soaking to prevent it from catching fire on the grill.

Preparing the Trout and Marinade:

1. Create the Marinade:

- In a bowl, combine the olive oil, minced garlic, fresh lemon juice, lemon zest, fresh thyme leaves, fresh rose- mary leaves, salt, and freshly ground black pepper.

- Mix the ingredients to create a fragrant marinade.

2. Marinate the Trout (Optional):

- Place the cleaned trout in a shallow dish.
- Pour the marinade over the trout, ensuring that both the inside and outside of the fish are coated.
- Cover the dish and refrigerate for 30 minutes if time allows, to infuse the flavors.

Grilling the Cedar Plank Trout:

1. Preheat the Grill:

- Preheat your grill to medium-high heat, around 375- 400°F (190-204°C) for indirect grilling.

2. Prepare the Cedar Plank:

- Remove the cedar plank from the water and pat it dry.
- Place the marinated trout on the soaked cedar plank, skin- side down.

3. Grill Over Indirect Heat:

- Place the cedar plank with the trout on the grill grates over indirect heat, away from direct flames.

4. Grill for 20-25 Minutes:

- Close the grill lid and grill the trout for about 20-25 minutes, or until the fish flakes easily and reaches an internal temperature of 145°F (63°C).

5. Garnish and Serve:

- Carefully remove the cedar plank with the grilled trout from the grill.
- Garnish with lemon slices and fresh herbs, if desired.

Serve your Cedar Plank Grilled Trout with a delightful smoky, woodsy flavor. The cedar plank infuses the fish with a unique aroma, making it a perfect dish for a special outdoor meal.

Grilled Mahi-Mahi with Mango Salsa

Preparation Time: 20 min | Marinating Time: 30 min | (optional) Cooking Time: 10-12 min
Servings: 4

Ingredients:
For the Grilled Mahi-Mahi:

- 4 mahi-mahi fillets (6-8 ounces each)
- 2 tablespoons olive oil
- 2 cloves garlic, minced
- 1 teaspoon ground cumin
- 1 teaspoon paprika
- Salt and freshly ground black pepper, to taste
- Lime wedges (for garnish, optional) For the Mango Salsa:
- 2 ripe mangoes, peeled, pitted, and diced
- 1/2 red onion, finely chopped
- 1 red bell pepper, diced
- 1/4 cup fresh cilantro, chopped
- 1 jalapeño pepper, seeded and minced (adjust to taste)
- 2 tablespoons fresh lime juice
- Salt and freshly ground black pepper, to taste

Instructions:
Preparing the Grilled Mahi-Mahi:

1. Create the Marinade (Optional):

- In a bowl, combine the olive oil, minced garlic, ground cumin, paprika, salt, and freshly ground black pepper.
- Mix the ingredients to create a flavorful marinade.

2. Marinate the Mahi-Mahi (Optional):

· Place the mahi-mahi fillets in a shallow dish.

· Pour the marinade over the fillets, ensuring they are well coated.

· Cover the dish and refrigerate for 30 minutes to let the flavors meld. You can skip marinating if you're short on time.

Grilling the Mahi-Mahi:

1. Preheat the Grill:

· Preheat your grill to medium-high heat, around 375- 400°F (190-204°C) for direct grilling.

2. Remove Mahi-Mahi from Marinade:

· Remove the mahi-mahi fillets from the marinade, allowing any excess marinade to drip off.

3. Season with Salt and Pepper:

· Season the mahi-mahi fillets with a pinch of salt and freshly ground black pepper to taste.

4. Grill the Mahi-Mahi:

· Place the mahi-mahi fillets on the preheated grill grates.

5. Grill for 5-6 Minutes per Side:

· Grill the mahi-mahi for about 5-6 minutes per side, or until the fish is opaque and flakes easily with a fork.

6. Check for Doneness:

· Ensure the mahi-mahi reaches an internal temperature of 145°F (63°C).

Preparing the Mango Salsa:

1. Create the Mango Salsa:

· In a bowl, combine the diced mangoes, finely chopped red onion, diced red bell pepper, chopped fresh cilantro, minced jalapeño pepper, fresh lime juice, salt, and freshly ground black pepper.

· Mix the ingredients well to create a fresh and fruity mango salsa.

Serving the Grilled Mahi-Mahi:

1. 1. Plate the Mahi-Mahi:

- Place the grilled mahi-mahi fillets on serving plates.

2. Top with Mango Salsa:

- Spoon the mango salsa generously over each mahi-mahi fillet.

3. Garnish and Serve:

- Garnish with lime wedges, if desired.

Enjoy your Grilled Mahi-Mahi with Mango Salsa, a delightful combination of tender grilled fish and a fresh, fruity mango salsa. It's a burst of flavor that's perfect for a light and delicious meal.

Grilled Tilapia with Lemon and Dill

Preparation Time: 10 min | Marinating Time: 30 min (optional) | Cooking Time: 8-10 min
Servings: 4

Ingredients:
For the Grilled Tilapia:

- 4 tilapia fillets (6-8 ounces each)
- 2 tablespoons olive oil
- 2 cloves garlic, minced
- 2 teaspoons fresh lemon juice
- 1 teaspoon fresh dill, chopped (or 1/2 teaspoon dried dill)
- Salt and freshly ground black pepper, to taste
- Lemon wedges (for garnish, optional)
- Fresh dill sprigs (for garnish, optional)

Instructions:
Preparing the Grilled Tilapia:

1. Create the Marinade (Optional):

- In a bowl, combine the olive oil, minced garlic, fresh lemon juice, chopped fresh dill (or dried dill), salt, and freshly ground black pepper.
- Mix the ingredients to create a light and refreshing mari- nade.

2. Marinate the Tilapia (Optional):

- Place the tilapia fillets in a shallow dish.
- Pour the marinade over the fillets, ensuring they are evenly coated.
- Cover the dish and refrigerate for 30 minutes to allow the flavors to meld. You can skip marinating if you're short on time.

Grilling the Tilapia:

1. Preheat the Grill:

- Preheat your grill to medium-high heat, around 375- 400°F (190-204°C) for direct grilling.

2. Remove Tilapia from Marinade (if marinated):

- Remove the tilapia fillets from the marinade, allowing any excess marinade to drip off.

3. Season with Salt and Pepper:

- Season the tilapia fillets with a pinch of salt and freshly ground black pepper to taste.

4. Grill the Tilapia:

- Place the tilapia fillets on the preheated grill grates.

5. Grill for 4-5 Minutes per Side:

- Grill the tilapia for about 4-5 minutes per side, or until the fish is opaque and flakes easily with a fork.

6. Check for Doneness:

- Ensure the tilapia reaches an internal temperature of 145°F (63°C).

Serving the Grilled Tilapia:

1. Plate the Tilapia:

- Place the grilled tilapia fillets on serving plates.

2. Garnish and Serve:

- Garnish with lemon wedges and fresh dill sprigs, if desired.

Enjoy your Grilled Tilapia with Lemon and Dill, a light and flaky dish that's bursting with the fresh and zesty flavors of lemon and dill. It's a quick and healthy meal that's perfect for any day of the week.

Grilled Swordfish Steaks with Olive Tapenade

Preparation Time: 20 min | Marinating Time: 30 min (optional) | Cooking Time: 10-12 min
Servings: 4

Ingredients:
For the Swordfish Steaks:

- 4 swordfish steaks (6-8 ounces each)
- 2 tablespoons olive oil
- 2 cloves garlic, minced
- 2 teaspoons fresh lemon juice
- 1 teaspoon fresh thyme leaves (or 1/2 teaspoon dried)
- Salt and freshly ground black pepper, to taste
- Lemon wedges (for garnish, optional)
- Fresh thyme sprigs (for garnish, optional) For the Olive Tapenade:
- 1 cup pitted Kalamata olives, chopped
- 2 tablespoons capers, drained and chopped
- 2 cloves garlic, minced
- 2 tablespoons fresh parsley, chopped
- 2 tablespoons fresh lemon juice
- 2 tablespoons extra-virgin olive oil
- 1 teaspoon Dijon mustard
- Freshly ground black pepper, to taste

Instructions:
Preparing the Swordfish Steaks:

1. Create the Marinade (Optional):

- In a bowl, combine the olive oil, minced garlic, fresh lemon juice, fresh thyme leaves (or dried thyme), salt, and freshly ground black pepper.
- Mix the ingredients to create a flavorful marinade.

197

2. Marinate the Swordfish (Optional):

- Place the swordfish steaks in a shallow dish.
- Pour the marinade over the steaks, ensuring they are well coated.
- Cover the dish and refrigerate for 30 minutes to let the flavors meld. You can skip marinating if you're short on time.

Grilling the Swordfish:

1. Preheat the Grill:

- Preheat your grill to medium-high heat, around 375- 400°F (190-204°C) for direct grilling.

2. Remove Swordfish from Marinade (if marinated):

- Remove the swordfish steaks from the marinade, allowing any excess marinade to drip off.

3. Season with Salt and Pepper:

- Season the swordfish steaks with a pinch of salt and freshly ground black pepper to taste.

4. Grill the Swordfish:

- Place the swordfish steaks on the preheated grill grates.

5. Grill for 4-5 Minutes per Side:

- Grill the swordfish for about 4-5 minutes per side, or until the fish is opaque and flakes easily with a fork.

6. Check for Doneness:

- Ensure the swordfish reaches an internal temperature of 145°F (63°C).

Preparing the Olive Tapenade:

1. Create the Olive Tapenade:

- In a bowl, combine the chopped Kalamata olives, capers, minced garlic, chopped fresh parsley, fresh lemon juice, extra-virgin olive oil, Dijon mustard, and freshly ground black pepper.
- Mix the ingredients well to create a savory olive tapenade.

Serving the Grilled Swordfish Steaks:

1. Plate the Swordfish:

- Place the grilled swordfish steaks on serving plates.

2. Top with Olive Tapenade:
- Spoon the olive tapenade generously over each swordfish steak.

3. Garnish and Serve:

- Garnish with lemon wedges and fresh thyme sprigs, if desired.

Enjoy your Grilled Swordfish Steaks with Olive Tapenade, featuring thick and succulent swordfish topped with a savory and flavorful olive tapenade. It's a gourmet-inspired dish that's perfect for a special dinner.

BBQ Glazed Grilled Scallops

Preparation Time: 15 min | Marinating Time: 15 min (optional) | Cooking Time: 6-8 min
Servings: 4

Ingredients:
For the BBQ Glaze:

- 1/2 cup barbecue sauce (use your favorite brand)
- 2 tablespoons honey
- 1 tablespoon apple cider vinegar
- 1 teaspoon Dijon mustard
- 1/2 teaspoon smoked paprika
- 1/4 teaspoon garlic powder
- Salt and freshly ground black pepper, to taste For the Scallops:
- 1 pound fresh scallops, cleaned and patted dry
- Olive oil for brushing
- Salt and freshly ground black pepper, to taste
- Fresh parsley or green onions (for garnish, optional)
- Lemon wedges (for garnish, optional)

Instructions:
Preparing the BBQ Glaze:

1. Create the BBQ Glaze:

- In a small saucepan, combine the barbecue sauce, honey, apple cider vinegar, Dijon mustard, smoked paprika, garlic powder, salt, and freshly ground black pepper.
- Heat the mixture over low heat, stirring occasionally, until it's well combined and slightly thickened, for about 5 minutes.
- Remove the glaze from heat and set it aside.

2. Marinate the Scallops (Optional):

- Place the scallops in a shallow dish.
- Pour half of the BBQ glaze over the scallops and gently toss to coat.

- Cover the dish and refrigerate for 15 minutes to let the flavors meld. You can skip marinating if you prefer.

Grilling the Scallops:

1. Preheat the Grill:

- Preheat your grill to medium-high heat, around 375- 400°F (190-204°C) for direct grilling.

2. Remove Scallops from Marinade (if marinated):

- Remove the scallops from the marinade, allowing any excess marinade to drip off.

3. Thread onto Skewers (Optional):

- If desired, thread the scallops onto skewers for easier grilling. Make sure to leave a small space between each scallop.

4. Brush with Olive Oil:

- Brush each side of the scallops lightly with olive oil to prevent sticking.

5. Season with Salt and Pepper:

- Season the scallops with a pinch of salt and freshly ground black pepper to taste.

6. Grill the Scallops:

- Place the scallops directly on the preheated grill grates.

7. Grill for 2-3 Minutes per Side:

- Grill the scallops for about 2-3 minutes per side, or until they are opaque and have grill marks.

8. Brush with BBQ Glaze:

- Brush the grilled scallops with the remaining BBQ glaze, turning them to coat all sides.

9. Caramelize the Glaze:

- Continue grilling the scallops for an additional 1-2 min- utes per side, brushing with more glaze as needed, until the glaze caramelizes and the scallops are cooked through.

Serving the BBQ Glazed Grilled Scallops:

1. Plate the Scallops:

- Transfer the grilled scallops to a serving platter.

2. Garnish and Serve:

- Garnish with fresh parsley or green onions and lemon wedges, if desired.

Enjoy your BBQ Glazed Grilled Scallops, featuring sweet and tangy glazed scallops with a delightful caramelized finish. It's a perfect appetizer or main course for any barbecue or seafood feast.

Herb-Butter Grilled Lobster Tails

Preparation Time: 15 min | Cooking Time: 10-12 min
Servings: 4

Ingredients:
For the Herb Butter:

- 1/2 cup unsalted butter, softened
- 2 cloves garlic, minced
- 1 tablespoon fresh parsley, finely chopped
- 1 tablespoon fresh chives, finely chopped
- 1 teaspoon fresh tarragon leaves, finely chopped (or 1/2 teaspoon dried)
- 1 teaspoon fresh thyme leaves, finely chopped (or 1/2 teaspoon dried)
- 1/2 teaspoon salt
- 1/4 teaspoon freshly ground black pepper
- Zest of 1 lemon
- 1 teaspoon fresh lemon juice For the Lobster Tails:
- 4 lobster tails (6-8 ounces each), thawed if frozen
- Olive oil for brushing
- Salt and freshly ground black pepper, to taste
- Lemon wedges (for garnish, optional)
- Fresh herbs (for garnish, optional)

Instructions:
Preparing the Herb Butter:

1. Create the Herb Butter:

- In a bowl, combine the softened butter, minced garlic, finely chopped fresh parsley, chives, tarragon, thyme, salt, freshly ground black pepper, lemon zest, and fresh lemon juice.
- Mix the ingredients thoroughly to create a flavorful herb butter.

2. Shape the Butter:

- Place the herb butter on a sheet of plastic wrap or parch- ment paper.
- Roll it into a log shape and twist the ends to seal.
- Refrigerate the herb butter until firm, for about 15-20 minutes.

Preparing the Lobster Tails:

1. Preheat the Grill:

- Preheat your grill to medium-high heat, around 375- 400°F (190-204°C) for direct grilling.

2. Prepare the Lobster Tails:

- Using kitchen shears or a sharp knife, cut along the top of each lobster tail shell, from the open end to the tail, without cutting through the tail meat.
- Carefully loosen the lobster meat from the shells, keeping it attached at the base. Lift the meat and lay it on top of the shells.

3. Brush with Olive Oil:

- Brush the lobster meat with olive oil to prevent sticking and promote a nice sear.

4. Season with Salt and Pepper:

- Season the lobster meat with a pinch of salt and freshly ground black pepper.

Grilling the Lobster Tails:

1. Slice and Grill the Herb Butter:

- Remove the herb butter log from the refrigerator.
- Slice it into thin rounds.

2. Add Herb Butter to Lobster Tails:

- Place the herb butter rounds on top of the lobster meat.

3. Grill for 5-6 Minutes per Side:

- Place the lobster tails on the preheated grill grates, meat side down.
- Grill for about 5-6 minutes on each side, or until the lobster meat is opaque and slightly charred, and the butter has melted into the meat.

4. Check for Doneness:

- Ensure the lobster meat reaches an internal temperature of 135°F (57°C).

Serving the Herb-Butter Grilled Lobster Tails:

1. Plate the Lobster Tails:

- Transfer the grilled lobster tails to serving plates.

2. Garnish and Serve:

- Garnish with lemon wedges and fresh herbs, if desired.

Enjoy your Herb-Butter Grilled Lobster Tails, featuring suc- culent lobster meat infused with the rich and aromatic flavors of herb butter. It's a luxurious and impressive dish for special occasions or a delightful seafood dinner.

Cajun-Style Grilled Shrimp and Sausage Skewers

Preparation Time: 20 min | Marinating Time: 30 min | Cooking Time: 8-10 min

Servings: 4

Ingredients:

For the Cajun Marinade:

1. 1/4 cup olive oil
2. 2 tablespoons Cajun seasoning
3. 2 cloves garlic, minced
4. 1 tablespoon fresh lemon juice
5. 1 teaspoon paprika
6. 1/2 teaspoon cayenne pepper (adjust to taste for spice)
7. Salt and freshly ground black pepper, to taste For the Shrimp and Sausage Skewers:
8. 1 pound large shrimp, peeled and deveined
9. 12-16 ounces spicy andouille sausage, cut into 1-inch thick slices
10. Wooden skewers (soaked in water for 30 minutes to prevent burning)
11. Lemon wedges (for garnish, optional)
12. Fresh parsley (for garnish, optional)

Instructions:

Preparing the Cajun Marinade:

1. Create the Cajun Marinade:

- In a bowl, combine the olive oil, Cajun seasoning, minced garlic, fresh lemon juice, paprika, cayenne pepper, salt, and freshly ground black pepper.
- Mix the ingredients thoroughly to create a flavorful Cajun marinade.

Marinating the Shrimp and Sausage:

1. Marinate the Shrimp and Sausage:

- Place the peeled and deveined shrimp and sliced andouille sausage in a large resealable plastic bag or a shallow dish.

2. Pour in the Marinade:

- Pour the Cajun marinade over the shrimp and sausage.

3. Seal and Marinate:

- Seal the bag (or cover the dish) and refrigerate for at least 30 minutes, allowing the flavors to meld. You can marinate longer for a stronger Cajun flavor.

Assembling and Grilling the Skewers:

1. Preheat the Grill:

- Preheat your grill to medium-high heat, around 375- 400°F (190-204°C) for direct grilling.

2. Thread the Skewers:

- Thread the marinated shrimp and andouille sausage alternately onto the wooden skewers, leaving a little space between each item.

3. Brush with Remaining Marinade:

- Brush the skewers with the remaining Cajun marinade to enhance the flavor.

4. Grill for 4-5 Minutes per Side:

- Place the skewers on the preheated grill grates.
- Grill for about 4-5 minutes per side, or until the shrimp are opaque and the sausage is slightly charred, and both are cooked through.

5. Check for Doneness:

- Ensure the shrimp have turned pink and the sausage is cooked.

Serving Cajun-Style Grilled Shrimp and Sausage Skewers:

1. Plate the Skewers:

· Transfer the grilled skewers to a serving platter.

2. Garnish and Serve:

· Garnish with lemon wedges and fresh parsley, if desired.

Enjoy your Cajun-Style Grilled Shrimp and Sausage Skewers, packed with the bold flavors of Cajun spices and the satisfying combination of shrimp and spicy andouille sausage. It's a taste of the South right from your grill!

Spicy Grilled Shrimp Skewers

Preparation Time: 15 min | Marinating Time: 30 min | Cooking Time: 4-6 min
Servings: 4

Ingredients:
For the Spicy Marinade:

- 1/4 cup olive oil
- 2 tablespoons fresh lime juice
- 2 cloves garlic, minced
- 1 teaspoon chili powder (adjust to taste)
- 1/2 teaspoon paprika
- 1/2 teaspoon cayenne pepper (adjust to taste)
- Salt and freshly ground black pepper, to taste
- Zest of 1 lime
- 1 tablespoon fresh cilantro, chopped (optional) For the Shrimp Skewers:
- 1 pound large shrimp, peeled and deveined
- Wooden skewers (soaked in water for 30 minutes to prevent burning)
- Lime wedges (for garnish, optional)
- Fresh cilantro leaves (for garnish, optional)

Instructions:
Preparing the Spicy Marinade:

1. Create the Spicy Marinade:

- In a bowl, combine the olive oil, fresh lime juice, minced garlic, chili powder, paprika, cayenne pepper, salt, freshly ground black pepper, lime zest, and chopped fresh cilantro (if using).
- Mix the ingredients thoroughly to create a zesty spicy marinade.

Marinating the Shrimp:

1. Marinate the Shrimp:

- Place the peeled and deveined shrimp in a large resealable plastic bag or a shallow dish.

2. Pour in the Marinade:

- Pour the spicy marinade over the shrimp.

3. Seal and Marinate:

- Seal the bag (or cover the dish) and refrigerate for at least 30 minutes, allowing the flavors to infuse. You can marinate longer for a spicier kick.

Assembling and Grilling the Skewers:

1. Preheat the Grill:

- Preheat your grill to medium-high heat, around 375- 400°F (190-204°C) for direct grilling.

2. Thread the Skewers:

- Thread the marinated shrimp onto the wooden skewers, leaving a little space between each shrimp.

3. Brush with Remaining Marinade:

- Brush the skewers with the remaining spicy marinade to enhance the flavor.

4. Grill for 2-3 Minutes per Side:

- Place the shrimp skewers on the preheated grill grates.
- Grill for about 2-3 minutes per side, or until the shrimp turn pink and are slightly charred. Be careful not to overcook, as shrimp cook quickly.

Serving Spicy Grilled Shrimp Skewers:

1. Plate the Skewers:

- Transfer the grilled shrimp skewers to a serving platter.

2. Garnish and Serve:

- Garnish with lime wedges and fresh cilantro leaves, if desired.

Enjoy your Spicy Grilled Shrimp Skewers, featuring succulent shrimp marinated in a zesty blend of chili, garlic, and lime. It's a perfect appetizer or main course for those who love a spicy kick!

Smoker Recipes: Beef

Classic Smoked Beef Brisket

Preparation Time: 15 min | Marinating Time: 8-12 hours (overnight)
Smoking Time: 10-12 hours | Resting Time: 1-2 hours
Servings: 8-10

Ingredients:
For the Brisket:

- 1 whole beef brisket, approximately 10-12 pounds
- 1/4 cup coarse kosher salt
- 1/4 cup black pepper, coarsely ground
- 2 tablespoons paprika
- 2 tablespoons garlic powder
- 2 tablespoons onion powder
- 1 tablespoon brown sugar
- 1 teaspoon cayenne pepper (adjust to your preferred level of spiciness)
- Wood chips or chunks for smoking (e.g., oak, hickory, or mesquite)

For Mop Sauce (optional):

- 1 cup beef broth or apple juice
- 1/4 cup Worcestershire sauce
- 1/4 cup cider vinegar
- 2 tablespoons olive oil

Instructions:
Preparing the Brisket:

1. Trim the Brisket: Start by trimming excess fat from the brisket, leaving a thin layer of fat (known as the fat cap) on top. This helps flavor and moisten the meat during smoking.

2. Create the Rub: In a bowl, combine the kosher salt, black pepper, paprika, garlic powder, onion powder, brown sugar, and cayenne pepper to create the rub.

3. Season the Brisket: Generously season the entire brisket with the rub, ensuring that all sides are evenly coated. Use your hands to press the rub into the meat, creating a flavorful crust. Wrap the brisket in plastic wrap and refrigerate it for at least 8-12 hours, or overnight.

Smoking the Brisket:

1. Preheat the Smoker: Preheat your smoker to a tempera- ture of 225-250°F (107-121°C). Use wood chips or chunks of your choice (oak, hickory, or mesquite) for smoke flavor.

2. Prepare the Mop Sauce (Optional): In a separate bowl, mix together the beef broth or apple juice, Worcester- shire sauce, cider vinegar, and olive oil to create a mop sauce. This can be used for basting during the smoking process to keep the brisket moist.

3. Place the Brisket in the Smoker: Place the seasoned brisket directly on the smoker grates with the fat cap facing up. If using a water pan in your smoker, fill it with water to help maintain a moist cooking environment.

4. Smoke the Brisket: Smoke the brisket at a consistent temperature of 225-250°F (107-121°C) for 10-12 hours, or until the internal temperature of the thickest part of the brisket reaches 195-203°F (90-95°C). This low and slow cooking process will ensure a tender and flavorful brisket.

5. Baste with Mop Sauce (Optional): If using the mop sauce, baste the brisket every 1-2 hours during the smoking process to add moisture and flavor.

6. Rest the Brisket: Once the brisket reaches the desired internal temperature, remove it from the smoker and wrap it in heavy-duty aluminum foil. Let it rest for 1-2 hours. This resting period allows the juices to redistribute, resulting in a juicy and tender brisket.

7. Slice and Serve: Slice the smoked beef brisket against the grain into thin slices. Serve it with your favorite bar- becue sauce, coleslaw, and pickles for a classic barbecue experience.

Enjoy your Classic Smoked Beef Brisket with family and friends. The long smoking time and flavorful rub create a mouthwatering, tender, and smoky brisket that's sure to be a hit at any barbecue gathering.

Smoked Beef Short Ribs

Preparation Time: 20 min | Marinating Time: 2-4 hours (optional) | Smoking Time: 5-6 hours
Resting Time: 20-30 min
Servings: 4-6

Ingredients:
For the Beef Ribs:

- 3-4 pounds of beef short ribs (about 2-3 racks)
- 1/4 cup coarse kosher salt
- 1/4 cup black pepper, coarsely ground
- 2 tablespoons smoked paprika
- 2 tablespoons garlic powder
- 2 tablespoons onion powder
- 1 tablespoon brown sugar
- 1 teaspoon cayenne pepper (adjust to your preferred level of spiciness)
- Wood chunks or chips for smoking (e.g., oak, hickory, or mesquite)

For the BBQ Sauce (optional):

- 1 cup of your favorite barbecue sauce

Instructions:
Preparing the Beef Ribs:

1. Trim the Ribs: Begin by trimming any excess fat and membrane from the beef ribs. Trimming helps the rub penetrate and the smoke flavor to infuse better.
2. Create the Rub: In a bowl, combine the kosher salt, black pepper, smoked paprika, garlic powder, onion powder, brown sugar, and cayenne pepper to create the rub.
3. Season the Ribs: Generously coat all sides of the beef ribs with the rub, ensuring even coverage. Use your hands to press the rub into the meat, creating a flavorful crust.
4. Marinating (Optional): If time allows, you can marinate the seasoned ribs in the refrigerator for 2-4 hours to allow the flavors to meld. This step is optional but enhances the taste.

Smoking the Beef Ribs:

1. Preheat the Smoker: Preheat your smoker to a tempera- ture of 225-250°F (107-121°C). Use wood chunks or chips of your choice (e.g., oak, hickory, or mesquite) for smoke flavor.

2. Place the Ribs in the Smoker: Place the seasoned beef ribs on the smoker grates, bone side down. If you have a water pan in your smoker, fill it with water to help maintain a moist cooking environment.

3. Smoke the Ribs: Smoke the beef ribs at a consistent temperature of 225-250°F (107-121°C) for 5-6 hours. You'll know they are done when the internal temperature of the meat reaches around 195-203°F (90-95°C) and the ribs are tender, and the meat has pulled back from the bones.

Optional BBQ Sauce Glaze:

1. Glaze with BBQ Sauce (Optional): In the last hour of smoking, you can brush the beef ribs with your favorite barbe-cue sauce if desired. Apply multiple thin coats for a sticky, flavorful glaze.

Resting and Serving:

1. Rest the Ribs: Once the beef ribs are done, remove them from the smoker and wrap them in heavy-duty aluminum foil. Allow them to rest for 20-30 minutes. This resting period lets the juices redistribute, resulting in moist and tender ribs.

2. Slice and Serve: After resting, carefully slice the beef ribs between the bones. They should be tender and practically falling off the bone.

3. Serve: Plate the smoked beef ribs and serve them with your favorite sides like coleslaw, cornbread, or grilled vegeta-bles.

Enjoy your Smoked Beef Ribs – a barbecue classic that's tender, smoky, and packed with rich flavor. Whether you prefer them sauced or with just the spice rub, these ribs are sure to be a crowd-pleaser at any barbecue gathering.

Smoked Beef Back Ribs

Preparation Time: 15 min | Marinating Time: 2-4 hours (optional) | Smoking Time: 4-6 hours
Resting Time: 20-30 min
Servings: 4-6

Ingredients:

For the Beef Back Ribs:

- 2-3 racks of beef back ribs (approximately 4-5 pounds)
- 1/4 cup coarse kosher salt
- 1/4 cup black pepper, coarsely ground
- 2 tablespoons paprika
- 2 tablespoons garlic powder
- 2 tablespoons onion powder
- 1 tablespoon brown sugar
- 1 teaspoon cayenne pepper (adjust to your preferred level of spiciness)
- Wood chunks or chips for smoking (e.g., oak, hickory, or mesquite)

Instructions:

Preparing the Beef Back Ribs:

1. Trim the Ribs: Start by trimming any excess fat and membrane from the beef back ribs. Trimming helps the rub penetrate and the smoke flavor to infuse better.

2. Create the Rub: In a bowl, combine the kosher salt, black pepper, paprika, garlic powder, onion powder, brown sugar, and cayenne pepper to create the rub.

3. Season the Ribs: Generously coat all sides of the beef back ribs with the rub, ensuring even coverage. Use your hands to press the rub into the meat, creating a flavorful crust.

4. Marinating (Optional): If time allows, you can marinate the seasoned ribs in the refrigerator for 2-4 hours to allow the flavors to meld. This step is optional but enhances the taste.

Smoking the Beef Back Ribs:

1. Preheat the Smoker: Preheat your smoker to a tempera- ture of 225-250°F (107-121°C). Use wood chunks or chips of your choice (e.g., oak, hickory, or mesquite) for smoke flavor.

2. Place the Ribs in the Smoker: Place the seasoned beef back ribs on the smoker grates, bone side down. If you have a water pan in your smoker, fill it with water to help maintain a moist cooking environment.

3. Smoke the Ribs: Smoke the beef back ribs at a consistent temperature of 225-250°F (107-121°C) for 4-6 hours. You'll know they are done when the meat is tender, and it easily pulls away from the bone.

Resting and Serving:

1. Rest the Ribs: Once the beef back ribs are done, remove them from the smoker and wrap them in heavy-duty aluminum foil. Allow them to rest for 20-30 minutes. This resting period lets the juices redistribute, resulting in moist and tender ribs.

2. Slice and Serve: After resting, carefully slice the beef back ribs between the bones. They should be tender and flavorful.

3. Serve: Plate the smoked beef back ribs and serve them with your favorite barbecue sides like coleslaw, baked beans, or cornbread.

Enjoy your Smoked Beef Back Ribs – a barbecue classic that's tender, smoky, and packed with rich flavor. These ribs are perfect for any BBQ gathering and sure to be a crowd-pleaser.

Smoked Prime Rib

Preparation Time: 30 minu | Smoking Time: Approximately 3-4 hours | Resting Time: 30 min
Servings: 8-10

Ingredients:
For the Prime Rib:

- 1 bone-in prime rib roast (about 5-6 pounds)
- 2 tablespoons olive oil
- 2 tablespoons coarsely ground black pepper
- 2 tablespoons kosher salt
- 1 tablespoon minced fresh rosemary (or 1 teaspoon dried rosemary)
- 1 tablespoon minced fresh thyme (or 1 teaspoon dried thyme)
- 6-8 cloves of garlic, minced

For the Smoker:

- Wood chips or chunks (hickory, oak, or mesquite work well)

Instructions:

1. Prepare the Prime Rib:

- Allow the prime rib roast to come to room temperature by placing it on the counter for about 1-2 hours before cooking.
- Preheat your smoker to a temperature of 225°F (110°C). Add your choice of wood chips or chunks for smoking flavor. For a milder smoke flavor, use fruitwood like apple or cherry. For a stronger smoky flavor, use hardwood like hickory or oak.

2. Season the Prime Rib:

- In a small bowl, combine the coarsely ground black pepper, kosher salt, minced rosemary, minced thyme, and minced garlic.
- Rub the entire surface of the prime rib with olive oil.
- Sprinkle the seasoning mixture evenly over the prime rib, pressing it into the meat to adhere.

3. Smoke the Prime Rib:

- Place the seasoned prime rib roast on the smoker grate, bone side down.
- Close the smoker and cook at 225°F (110°C) until the internal temperature of the prime rib reaches your desired level of doneness:
- Rare: 120-125°F (49-52°C)
- Medium Rare: 130-135°F (54-57°C)
- Medium: 140-145°F (60-63°C)
- Medium Well: 150-155°F (66-68°C)
- Well Done: 160°F (71°C) or higher

4. Rest the Prime Rib:

- Once the prime rib reaches your desired internal temper- ature, remove it from the smoker and place it on a cutting board.
- Tent the prime rib loosely with aluminum foil and let it rest for about 30 minutes. This allows the juices to redistribute, resulting in a juicier roast.

5. Carve and Serve:

- After resting, carve the smoked prime rib into thick slices. Serve it with your favorite sides and enjoy!

Smoking a prime rib infuses it with a delicious smoky flavor, making it a fantastic choice for special occasions and holiday dinners. Adjust the smoking time to achieve your preferred level of doneness, and be sure to use a meat thermometer for accuracy.

Smoked Beef Tenderloin

Preparation Time: 15 min | Marinating Time: 2-4 hours (optional) | Smoking Time: 1-2 hours

Resting Time: 20-30 min

Servings: 4-6

Ingredients:

For the Beef Tenderloin:

- 2-3 pounds of beef tenderloin (whole)
- 1/4 cup olive oil
- 2 tablespoons coarse kosher salt
- 2 tablespoons black pepper, coarsely ground
- 2 tablespoons garlic powder
- 2 tablespoons dried rosemary (or your preferred herbs)
- Wood chunks or chips for smoking (e.g., oak, hickory, or cherry)

Instructions:

Preparing the Beef Tenderloin:

1. Trim the Tenderloin: Start by trimming any excess fat or silver skin from the beef tenderloin. The goal is to have a clean, even surface.

2. Marinating (Optional): In a bowl, combine the olive oil, coarse kosher salt, black pepper, garlic powder, and dried rosemary (or your preferred herbs) to create a marinade. You can choose to marinate the tenderloin in this mixture for 2-4 hours in the refrigerator to enhance the flavor.

Smoking the Beef Tenderloin:

1. Preheat the Smoker: Preheat your smoker to a low temperature of 200-225°F (93-107°C). Use wood chunks or chips of your choice (e.g., oak, hickory, or cherry) for smoke flavor.

2. Prepare the Tenderloin: Remove the beef tenderloin from the marinade and let any excess marinade drip off. Pat the tenderloin dry with paper towels.

3. Smoke the Tenderloin: Place the prepared beef tender- loin on the smoker grates. Insert a meat thermometer probe into the thickest part of the tenderloin to monitor the internal temperature.

4. Smoke at Low Temperature: Smoke the beef tenderloin at the low smoker temperature of 200-225°F (93-107°C) for 1-2 hours, or until it reaches your desired level of doneness. Aim for an internal temperature of 130-135°F (54-57°C) for medium-rare or adjust to your preference.

5. Rest the Tenderloin: Once the tenderloin reaches the desired temperature, remove it from the smoker and tent it loosely with aluminum foil. Allow it to rest for 20-30 minutes. This resting period lets the juices redistribute, resulting in a juicy and tender tenderloin.

Slicing and Serving:

1. Slice and Serve: After resting, carefully slice the smoked beef tenderloin into 1/2-inch-thick medallions. Arrange the slices on a serving platter.

2. Optional Sauce: If desired, you can serve the smoked beef tenderloin with a sauce of your choice, such as a horseradish cream sauce or a red wine reduction.

3. Enjoy: Serve your smoked beef tenderloin as a luxurious main course. It's a tender and flavorful dish that's perfect for special occasions or any time you want to impress your guests.

This Smoked Beef Tenderloin recipe is a fantastic way to enjoy the tenderness and rich flavor of this premium cut with a smoky twist.

Smoked Tri-Tip with Santa Maria-Style Rub

Preparation Time: 15 min | Marinating Time: 2-4 hours | Smoking Time: 1-1.5 hours
Resting Time: 20-30 min
Servings: 4-6

Ingredients:
For the Tri-Tip:

- 2-3 pounds of tri-tip roast
- Santa Maria-style rub (recipe below)
- Wood chunks or chips for smoking (e.g., oak or mesquite) For the Santa

Maria-Style Rub:

- 2 tablespoons kosher salt
- 1 tablespoon black pepper, coarsely ground
- 1 tablespoon garlic powder
- 1 tablespoon onion powder
- 1 tablespoon paprika (preferably smoked)
- 1 teaspoon cayenne pepper (adjust to your preferred level of spiciness)

For Serving (Optional):
- Santa Maria-style salsa (recipe below)
- Sliced French bread or garlic bread

Instructions:
Preparing the Santa Maria-Style Rub:

1. Create the Rub: In a bowl, combine the kosher salt, black pepper, garlic powder, onion powder, paprika, and cayenne pepper to create the Santa Maria-style rub. This rub is a classic for tri-tip and adds incredible flavor.

Preparing the Tri-Tip:

1. Trim and Season: Trim any excess fat and silver skin from the tri-tip roast. Generously season all sides of the tri-tip with the Santa Maria-style rub, ensuring an even coating. Press the rub into the meat for better adherence.
2. Marinate (Optional): Place the seasoned tri-tip in a resealable plastic bag or dish and marinate it in the refrigerator for 2-4 hours to allow the flavors to meld. While marinating is optional, it enhances the taste.

Smoking the Tri-Tip:

1. Preheat the Smoker: Preheat your smoker to a tempera- ture of 225-250°F (107-121°C). Use wood chunks or chips of your choice (e.g., oak or mesquite) for smoke flavor.

2. Smoke the Tri-Tip: Place the seasoned tri-tip on the smoker grates. Insert a meat thermometer probe into the thickest part of the tri-tip to monitor the internal temperature.

3. Smoke at Medium-Rare: Smoke the tri-tip at a consis- tent temperature of 225-250°F (107-121°C) for approxi- mately 1-1.5 hours, or until it reaches an internal temper- ature of 130-135°F (54-57°C) for medium-rare. Adjust the cooking time for your preferred level of doneness.

Resting and Slicing:

1. Rest the Tri-Tip: Once the tri-tip reaches the desired temperature, remove it from the smoker and tent it loosely with aluminum foil. Allow it to rest for 20-30 minutes. This resting period lets the juices redistribute, resulting in a juicy and tender tri-tip.

2. Slicing: After resting, slice the smoked tri-tip against the grain into thin, angled slices. This ensures tender- ness and optimal flavor.

Serving:

1. Serve: Plate the sliced smoked tri-tip, and if desired, serve it with Santa Maria-style salsa and sliced French bread or garlic bread. Enjoy the delicious flavors of Santa Maria-style barbecue!

Santa Maria-Style Salsa:
Ingredients:

- 2 tomatoes, diced
- 1/2 cup red onion, finely chopped
- 1/4 cup fresh cilantro, chopped
- 2 cloves garlic, minced
- 2 tablespoons red wine vinegar
- 2 tablespoons olive oil
- Salt and pepper to taste

Instructions:

1. In a bowl, combine all the salsa ingredients and mix well.
2. Allow the salsa to sit for about 30 minutes before serving to allow the flavors to meld.

Serve your Smoked Tri-Tip with Santa Maria-style rub and salsa for a mouthwatering and authentic barbecue experience. It's a flavorful and tender dish that's sure to impress your guests!

Smoked Barbacoa Tacos

Preparation Time: 20 min | Smoking Time: 4-5 hours | Resting Time: 15 min
ervings: 6-8

Ingredients:
For the Smoked Barbacoa:

- 4-5 pounds beef cheek or beef chuck roast
- Wood chunks or chips for smoking (mesquite or oak work well)
- Salt and black pepper, to taste
- 2 tablespoons vegetable oil
- 1 large onion, chopped
- 4 cloves garlic, minced
- 2-3 chipotle peppers in adobo sauce (adjust to your preferred level of spiciness)
- 2 teaspoons ground cumin
- 2 teaspoons dried oregano
- 1 teaspoon ground coriander
- 1 teaspoon ground cloves
- 1/2 cup beef broth For the Drippings Sauce:
- Drippings from the smoked barbacoa
- 1/2 cup beef broth
- 2 tablespoons lime juice
- 2 tablespoons chopped fresh cilantro
- Salt and black pepper, to taste For Serving:
- Corn or flour tortillas
- Sliced red onions
- Chopped fresh cilantro
- Lime wedges
- Salsa (optional)

Instructions:

Smoking the Barbacoa:

1. Preheat the Smoker: Preheat your smoker to a low and steady temperature of 225-250°F (107-121°C). Use wood chunks or chips for smoke flavor. Mesquite or oak wood can add a robust smoky flavor.

2. Season the Meat: Season the beef cheek or chuck roast generously with salt and black pepper on all sides.

3. Sear the Meat (Optional): Heat the vegetable oil in a large skillet over high heat. Sear the seasoned meat on all sides until it develops a rich, brown crust. This step is optional but can add extra flavor.

4. Smoke the Meat: Once the smoker is ready, place the seasoned meat directly on the smoker grates. Insert a meat thermometer probe into the thickest part of the meat.

5. Smoke Low and Slow: Smoke the meat at a consistent temperature of 225-250°F (107-121°C) for about 4-5 hours or until the internal temperature reaches around 195-203°F (90-95°C). The meat should be tender and easy to shred.

Resting and Shredding:

1. Rest the Smoked Meat: Remove the smoked meat from the smoker and let it rest for about 15 minutes. This allows the juices to redistribute and keeps the meat moist.

2. Shred the Barbacoa: Use two forks or your hands to shred the smoked barbacoa into bite-sized pieces. Set aside.

Making the Drippings Sauce:

1. Collect the Drippings: Collect the drippings from the smoked barbacoa that accumulated in the smoker's drip pan.

2. Combine with Other Ingredients: In a saucepan, com- bine the collected drippings, beef broth, lime juice, and chopped cilantro. Bring the mixture to a simmer over medium heat and cook for a few minutes. Taste and adjust the seasoning with salt and black pepper if needed.

Serving:

1. Serve the Barbacoa Tacos: Warm the tortillas and fill them with the shredded smoked barbacoa. Top with sliced red onions, chopped cilantro, and a squeeze of fresh lime juice. Drizzle the drippings sauce over the tacos and add salsa if desired.

Enjoy your Smoked Barbacoa Tacos with a rich and flavorful sauce made from the drippings, creating a truly irresistible taco experience!

Smoked Quesabirria Tacos

Preparation Time: 20 min | Marinating Time: 2-4 hours | Smoking Time: 4-6 hours
Servings: 4-6 (for tacos)

Ingredients:
For the Smoked Quesabirria:

Smoked Birria Tacos Recipe

Birria, traditionally a savory, hearty Mexican stew, is given a twist in this recipe by incorporating the rich, deep flavors achieved through smoking. These smoked birria tacos are not only packed with flavor but also provide a delightful textural contrast with crispy tortillas and tender, juicy meat.

Ingredients
For the Birria:

- 3 lbs beef chuck roast or brisket
- Salt and pepper, to taste
- 3 dried guajillo chiles
- 2 dried ancho chiles
- 1 dried chipotle chile
- 4 cups beef broth
- 1 medium onion, chopped
- 6 cloves garlic
- 1 cinnamon stick
- 1 tsp ground cumin
- 1 tsp dried oregano
- 1/2 tsp ground cloves
- 1/2 tsp ground ginger
- 2 bay leaves
- 3 tbsp apple cider vinegar

For the Tacos:

- Corn tortillas
- Chopped cilantro
- Diced onion
- Lime wedges

229

- Shredded cheese (optional)

Instructions

1. Prepare the Meat:

- Season the beef liberally with salt and pepper.
- Preheat your smoker to 250°F (120°C).
- Smoke the beef for 3-4 hours until it develops a deep, smoky flavor and a nice crust.

2. Prepare the Chile Sauce:

- While the beef is smoking, toast the dried chiles in a dry skillet until fragrant. Remove stems and seeds.
- In a pot, add the toasted chiles and beef broth. Bring to a boil, then simmer for 15 minutes.
- Blend the chile and broth mixture with onion, garlic, cinnamon, cumin, oregano, cloves, ginger, and apple cider vinegar until smooth.

3. Combine and Cook:

- Once the beef is smoked, transfer it to a large pot.
- Add the chile sauce and bay leaves to the pot with the beef.
- Simmer on low heat for 2-3 hours until the beef is ex- tremely tender and the flavors meld together.

4. Shred the Meat:

- Remove the beef from the pot and shred it with two forks.
- Skim off any excess fat from the surface of the sauce.

5. Assemble the Tacos:

- Dip corn tortillas in the birria sauce and place them on a hot griddle or skillet.
- Add shredded cheese (if using) and allow it to melt.
- Add shredded beef on top of the cheese.
- Fold the tortillas and cook until crispy.

6. Serve:

- Serve your smoked birria tacos with fresh chopped cilantro, diced onion, and a squeeze of lime.
- Use the remaining birria sauce as a dipping broth for the tacos.

Enjoy this smoky, savory, and utterly delicious take on the classic birria tacos, perfect for a unique and memorable meal.

Smoker Recipes: Pork

Classic Pulled Pork

Preparation Time: 15 minutes | Marinating Time: 8-12 hours (overnight) | Smoking Time: 10-12 hours

Resting Time: 1-2 hours

Servings: 10-12

Ingredients:

For the Pork:

- 1 whole pork shoulder (Boston butt), 8-10 pounds
- 1/4 cup yellow mustard (for binding the rub)
- 1/4 cup apple cider vinegar (for spritzing during smoking)
- Wood chunks or chips for smoking (hickory, apple, or cherry are great choices)

For the Spice Rub:

- 1/4 cup paprika
- 2 tablespoons brown sugar
- 2 tablespoons kosher salt
- 1 tablespoon black pepper
- 1 tablespoon garlic powder
- 1 tablespoon onion powder
- 1 tablespoon ground cumin
- 1 tablespoon chili powder
- 1 teaspoon cayenne pepper (adjust to your preferred level of spiciness)

For Serving:

- Burger buns or sandwich rolls
- Coleslaw (optional)
- BBQ sauce (your favorite variety)

Instructions:

Preparing the Spice Rub:

1. Combine Ingredients: In a bowl, combine all the spice rub ingredients: paprika, brown sugar, kosher salt, black pepper, garlic powder, onion powder, ground cumin, chili powder, and cayenne pepper. Mix well to create a flavorful rub.

Preparing the Pork:

2. Trim Excess Fat: Examine the pork shoulder and trim any excess fat from the surface. Leave a thin layer of fat to add flavor and moisture.

3. Mustard Coating: Using a brush or your hands, coat the entire pork shoulder with a thin layer of yellow mustard. This will help the rub adhere to the meat.

4. Apply the Spice Rub: Generously apply the spice rub to all sides of the pork shoulder, pressing it into the meat to create a flavorful crust. Make sure to cover the entire surface.

5. Wrap and Refrigerate: Wrap the seasoned pork shoulder in plastic wrap or aluminum foil and refrigerate it for 8-12 hours or overnight. This allows the flavors to penetrate the meat.

Smoking the Pork:

1. Preheat the Smoker: Preheat your smoker to a low and steady temperature of 225-250°F (107-121°C). Use wood chunks or chips of your choice for smoke flavor.

2. Place the Pork Shoulder: Place the seasoned pork shoul- der in the smoker, fat side up. Insert a meat thermometer probe into the thickest part of the meat.

3. Smoke Low and Slow: Smoke the pork shoulder at a consistent temperature of 225-250°F (107-121°C) for 10- 12 hours, or until it reaches an internal temperature of 195-203°F (90-95°C). This is the ideal temperature for tender and easily pulled pork.

4. Spritz with Apple Cider Vinegar: During the smoking process, occasionally spritz the pork shoulder with apple cider vinegar to keep it moist and add a hint of acidity.

5. Rest the Pork: Once the pork reaches the desired tem- perature, remove it from the smoker and let it rest for 1-2 hours. Place it in a large aluminum foil pan, cover it with foil, and allow it to rest. This rest helps the juices redistribute and makes the meat even more tender.

Pulling and Serving:

1. Pull the Pork: Using two forks or meat claws, shred the smoked pork shoulder into bite-sized pieces. The meat should easily fall apart.

2. Serve: Serve the pulled pork on burger buns or sandwich rolls. You can top it with coleslaw and your favorite BBQ sauce for added flavor and texture.

3. Enjoy: Enjoy your Classic Pulled Pork sandwiches, a true BBQ classic that's tender, smoky, and full of flavor!

Classic Pulled Pork is a crowd-pleasing favorite, and it's perfect for gatherings and cookouts. Savor the tender, smoky goodness in each bite.

Applewood Smoked Pork Loin with Apple Cider Glaze

Preparation Time: 15 min | Smoking Time: 2-3 hours | Resting Time: 15 min
Servings: 6-8

Ingredients:

For the Pork Loin:

- 1 pork loin roast, approximately 3-4 pounds
- 2 tablespoons olive oil
- 2 tablespoons Dijon mustard
- 2 tablespoons brown sugar
- 1 tablespoon smoked paprika
- 1 teaspoon garlic powder
- 1 teaspoon onion powder
- 1 teaspoon dried thyme
- 1 teaspoon salt
- 1/2 teaspoon black pepper
- Applewood chunks or chips for smoking For the Apple Cider Glaze:
- 1 cup apple cider
- 1/4 cup apple cider vinegar
- 1/4 cup brown sugar
- 2 tablespoons Dijon mustard
- 1 tablespoon cornstarch (optional, for thickening)

Instructions:

Preparing the Pork Loin:

1. Trim the Pork Loin: Examine the pork loin and trim any excess fat or silver skin from the surface. Pat it dry with paper towels.

2. Prepare the Rub: In a small bowl, combine the smoked paprika, brown sugar, garlic powder, onion powder, dried thyme, salt, and black pepper to create the rub.

3. Coat with Mustard and Rub: Brush the pork loin with olive oil to help the rub adhere. Next, spread a layer of Dijon mustard evenly over the entire surface of the pork loin. Sprinkle the rub evenly over the mustard-coated pork loin, pressing it onto the meat to create a flavorful crust.

Smoking the Pork Loin:

1. Preheat the Smoker: Preheat your smoker to a low and steady temperature of 225-250°F (107-121°C). Use applewood chunks or chips for smoke flavor.

2. Smoke the Pork Loin: Place the seasoned pork loin in the smoker, making sure to insert a meat thermometer probe into the thickest part of the meat.

3. Smoke at Low Temperature: Smoke the pork loin at a consistent temperature of 225-250°F (107-121°C) for approximately 2-3 hours, or until the internal temper- ature reaches 145-150°F (63-66°C). This is the ideal temperature for a juicy and slightly pink center.

Preparing the Apple Cider Glaze:

1. Combine Ingredients: In a saucepan, combine the ap- ple cider, apple cider vinegar, brown sugar, and Dijon mustard. Bring the mixture to a boil over medium heat.

2. Thicken the Glaze (Optional): If you prefer a thicker glaze, you can whisk in 1 tablespoon of cornstarch mixed with 2 tablespoons of cold water. Continue to simmer until the glaze thickens to your desired consistency.

3. Simmer and Reduce: Reduce the heat to low and let the glaze simmer for about 10-15 minutes, or until it has reduced by half. Stir occasionally to prevent burning.

Resting and Serving:

1. Rest the Pork Loin: Once the pork loin reaches the desired temperature, remove it from the smoker and let it rest for 15 minutes. This resting period allows the juices to redistribute.

2. Slice and Glaze: Slice the smoked pork loin into thick slices and drizzle the apple cider glaze over the top.

3. Serve: Serve the Applewood Smoked Pork Loin with Apple Cider Glaze as the centerpiece of your meal, ac- companied by your favorite sides. The subtly sweet applewood smoke and apple cider glaze complement the pork loin beautifully.

Enjoy your Applewood Smoked Pork Loin with its subtly sweet, smoky flavor and delightful apple cider glaze – a perfect dish for any occasion!

Maple-Bourbon Smoked Pork Tenderloin

Preparation Time: 15 min | Marinating Time: 2-4 hours | Smoking Time: 1-1.5 hours

Resting Time: 10 min

Servings: 4

Ingredients:

For the Pork Tenderloin:

- 2 pork tenderloins (about 1 to 1.5 pounds each)
- Wood chunks or chips for smoking (apple, cherry, or pecan work well)

For the Maple-Bourbon Marinade:

- 1/2 cup pure maple syrup
- 1/4 cup bourbon whiskey
- 2 tablespoons Dijon mustard
- 2 cloves garlic, minced
- 1 teaspoon smoked paprika
- 1/2 teaspoon salt
- 1/2 teaspoon black pepper

Instructions:

Preparing the Maple-Bourbon Marinade:

1. Combine Marinade Ingredients: In a bowl, whisk together the pure maple syrup, bourbon whiskey, Dijon mustard, minced garlic, smoked paprika, salt, and black pepper. This will be your flavorful marinade.

Marinating the Pork Tenderloin:

1. Marinate the Pork: Place the pork tenderloins in a resealable plastic bag or a shallow dish. Pour the maple-bourbon marinade over the pork tenderloins, ensuring they are fully coated. Seal the bag or cover the dish and refrigerate for 2-4 hours. Marinating allows the pork to absorb the sweet and savory flavors.

Smoking the Pork Tenderloin:

1. Preheat the Smoker: Preheat your smoker to a low and steady temperature of 225-250°F (107-121°C). Use wood chunks or chips for smoke flavor. Apple, cherry, or pecan wood complements the maple and bourbon flavors nicely.

2. Prepare the Pork Tenderloins: Remove the pork tender- loins from the marinade and allow any excess marinade to drip off. Discard the marinade.

3. Place on the Smoker: Once the smoker is ready, place the pork tenderloins directly on the smoker grates.

4. Smoke Low and Slow: Smoke the pork tenderloins at a consistent temperature of 225-250°F (107-121°C) for about 1-1.5 hours. The internal temperature of the pork tenderloins should reach 145-150°F (63-66°C) for safe consumption.

Resting and Serving:

1. Rest the Pork Tenderloin: Remove the smoked pork tenderloins from the smoker and let them rest for about 10 minutes. This allows the juices to redistribute and keeps the meat moist and tender.

2. Slice and Serve: Slice the smoked Maple-Bourbon Pork Tenderloin into thick, juicy portions. Serve it as the centerpiece of your meal, accompanied by your favorite sides, such as roasted vegetables or a green salad.

Enjoy your Maple-Bourbon Smoked Pork Tenderloin, fea- turing a perfect balance of sweet maple and smoky bourbon flavors that make every bite a delightful experience!

Stuffed Pork Loin

Preparation Time: 20 min | Cooking Time: 1 hour | Resting Time: 10 min
Servings: 4-6

Ingredients:
For the Pork Loin:

- 2-3 pounds boneless pork loin roast
- Salt and black pepper, to taste
- 2 tablespoons olive oil

For the Stuffing:

- 1 cup fresh spinach, chopped
- 1 cup mushrooms, finely chopped
- 1 small onion, finely chopped
- 2 cloves garlic, minced
- 1/2 cup shredded mozzarella cheese
- 1/4 cup grated Parmesan cheese
- 2 tablespoons olive oil
- Salt and black pepper, to taste For the Seasoning Rub:
- 1 tablespoon paprika
- 1 teaspoon dried thyme
- 1 teaspoon dried rosemary
- 1 teaspoon dried sage
- 1/2 teaspoon garlic powder
- 1/2 teaspoon onion powder
- Salt and black pepper, to taste

Instructions:

Preparing the Pork Loin:

1. Preheat the Oven: Preheat your oven to 350°F (175°C).

2. Butterfly the Pork Loin: Lay the pork loin roast on a cutting board. Using a sharp knife, butterfly the pork loin by making a horizontal cut lengthwise, about 1 inch from the bottom of the roast, stopping about half an inch from the other side. Open up the pork loin like a book and lay it flat.

3. Pound and Season: Place a sheet of plastic wrap over the butterflied pork loin and gently pound it with a meat mallet or rolling pin to even out the thickness. Season both sides of the pork loin with salt and black pepper.

Preparing the Stuffing:

1. Sauté Vegetables: In a large skillet, heat 2 tablespoons of olive oil over medium heat. Add the chopped mushrooms, onion, and garlic. Sauté for about 5 minutes, or until the vegetables have softened and any excess moisture has evaporated. Season with salt and black pepper.

2. Add Spinach and Cheese: Add the chopped spinach to the skillet and cook for an additional 2-3 minutes until wilted. Remove the skillet from heat and stir in the shredded mozzarella and grated Parmesan cheese. Allow the cheese to melt slightly.

3. Stuff the Pork Loin: Spread the mushroom and spinach mixture evenly over the butterflied pork loin, leaving a border of about 1 inch around the edges. Carefully roll up the pork loin, starting from the long side, to encase the stuffing. Use kitchen twine to tie the stuffed pork loin at 1-inch intervals to secure it.

Seasoning and Roasting:

1. Prepare the Seasoning Rub: In a small bowl, combine the paprika, dried thyme, dried rosemary, dried sage, garlic powder, onion powder, salt, and black pepper to create the seasoning rub.

2. Season the Pork Loin: Brush the outside of the stuffed pork loin with 2 tablespoons of olive oil. Rub the season- ing mixture evenly over the entire surface of the pork loin.

Roasting:

1. Roast the Pork Loin: Place the seasoned stuffed pork loin on a roasting pan or a baking sheet with a wire rack. Roast in the preheated oven for approximately 45 minutes to 1 hour, or until the internal temperature reaches 145-150°F (63-66°C) and the pork loin is cooked through.

2. Rest and Slice: Remove the stuffed pork loin from the oven and let it rest for about 10 minutes before slicing. This allows the juices to redistribute and keeps the meat moist.

3. Slice and Serve: Slice the stuffed pork loin into thick slices and serve it as the centerpiece of your meal. You can also make a gravy or sauce using the pan drippings if desired.

Enjoy your delicious Stuffed Pork Loin, filled with savory mushrooms, spinach, and cheese, seasoned to perfection!

Smoked Pork Chops

Preparation Time: 20 min | Brining Time: 2-4 hours | Smoking Time: 1-2 hours
Resting Time: 10 min
Servings: 4

Ingredients:
For the Pork Chops:

- 4 thick-cut bone-in pork chops (about 1 to 1.5 inches thick)
- Wood chunks or chips for smoking (apple or hickory work well)

For the Brine:

- 4 cups cold water
- 1/4 cup kosher salt
- 1/4 cup brown sugar
- 2 cloves garlic, minced
- 1 bay leaf
- 1 teaspoon black peppercorns For the Seasoning (optional):
- Your favorite pork rub or seasoning blend

Instructions:
Preparing the Brine:

1. Combine Brine Ingredients: In a large bowl, combine cold water, kosher salt, brown sugar, minced garlic, bay leaf, and black peppercorns. Stir until the salt and sugar are fully dissolved.

2. Brine the Pork Chops: Place the pork chops in a large resealable plastic bag or a shallow dish. Pour the brine mixture over the pork chops, ensuring they are fully submerged. Seal the bag or cover the dish and refrigerate for 2-4 hours. Brining helps keep the pork chops moist and enhances their flavor.

Smoking the Pork Chops:

1. Preheat the Smoker: Preheat your smoker to a low and steady temperature of 225-250°F (107-121°C). Use wood chunks or chips for smoke flavor. Apple or hickory wood pairs nicely with pork.

2. Season the Pork Chops (Optional): If you prefer, you can season the pork chops with your favorite pork rub or seasoning blend at this point. Make sure to season both sides evenly.

3. Place on the Smoker: Once the smoker is ready, remove the pork chops from the brine and pat them dry with paper towels. Place the pork chops on the smoker grates.

4. Smoke Low and Slow: Smoke the pork chops at a consistent temperature of 225-250°F (107-121°C) for 1-2 hours, depending on their thickness. The internal temperature of the pork chops should reach about 145-150°F (63-66°C) for a juicy and safe result.

Resting and Serving:

1. Rest the Pork Chops: Remove the smoked pork chops from the smoker and let them rest for about 10 minutes. This allows the juices to redistribute and keeps the meat tender.

2. Serve: Serve the smoked pork chops as the centerpiece of your meal, accompanied by your favorite sides, such as mashed potatoes, grilled vegetables, or a fresh salad.

Enjoy your Smoked Pork Chops, which are not only flavorful but also tender and succulent thanks to the brining process and the aromatic smoke infusion from the smoker!

Smoked Stuffed Pork Chops

Preparatiime: 20 min | Smoking Time: 2-3 hours

Servings: 4

Ingredients:

For the Stuffed Pork Chops:

- 4 thick-cut boneless pork chops
- 4 ounces cream cheese, softened
- 1-2 jalapeños, finely chopped (adjust to your preferred level of spiciness)
- 1 cup fresh spinach, chopped
- 2 cloves garlic, minced
- 1/2 cup shredded cheddar cheese (optional)
- Salt and pepper to taste
- Toothpicks (for securing the chops)
- Olive oil (for brushing) For the Pork Chop Rub:
- 1 tablespoon paprika
- 1 teaspoon garlic powder
- 1 teaspoon onion powder
- 1 teaspoon dried thyme
- 1 teaspoon dried oregano
- 1/2 teaspoon salt
- 1/2 teaspoon black pepper

Instructions:

Preparing the Stuffed Pork Chops:

1. Prepare the Filling: In a bowl, combine the softened cream cheese, chopped jalapeños, chopped spinach, minced garlic, and shredded cheddar cheese (if using). Mix well until all the ingredients are evenly incorporated. Season with salt and pepper to taste.

2. Butterfly the Pork Chops: To create a pocket for the filling, butterfly each pork chop by making a horizontal cut along the side, being careful not to cut all the way through. Open up the pocket and flatten the chop slightly with a meat mallet.

3. Stuff the Pork Chops: Generously fill each butterflied pork chop with the cream cheese, jalapeño, and spinach mixture. Be sure not to overstuff them; you should be able to fold them closed.

4. Secure with Toothpicks: Use toothpicks to secure the stuffed pork chops, ensuring that the filling remains inside during the smoking process.

Preparing the Pork Chop Rub:

1. Create the Rub: In a small bowl, combine the paprika, garlic powder, onion powder, dried thyme, dried oregano, salt, and black pepper to create the pork chop rub.

2. Season the Pork Chops: Brush each stuffed pork chop with a little olive oil and season both sides with the pork chop rub, ensuring they are evenly coated.

Smoking the Stuffed Pork Chops:

1. Preheat the Smoker: Preheat your smoker to a tempera- ture of 225-250°F (107-121°C). Use wood chunks or chips of your choice (e.g., applewood or hickory) for smoke flavor.

2. Smoke the Chops: Place the seasoned and stuffed pork chops on the smoker grates. Insert a meat thermometer probe into one of the chops to monitor the internal temperature.

3. Smoke at Low Temperature: Smoke the stuffed pork chops at a consistent temperature of 225-250°F (107- 121°C) for approximately 2-3 hours, or until they reach an internal temperature of 145-150°F (63-66°C) for medium done-ness. Ensure the thermometer probe is inserted into the center of one of the chops to get an accurate reading.

4. Rest and Serve: Once the pork chops reach the desired temperature, remove them from the smoker and let them rest for a few minutes. This allows the juices to redistribute.

5. Serve: Serve the Smoked Stuffed Pork Chops with cream cheese, jalapeño, and spinach as a delicious and flavorful main course. Consider garnishing with fresh chopped herbs or extra jalapeño slices for added flavor and pre- sentation.

Enjoy your Smoked Stuffed Pork Chops with a delightful cream cheese, jalapeño, and spinach filling, all infused with smoky goodness from the grill!

Smoked Pork Ribs

Preparation Time: 20 min | Marinating Time: 2-4 hours (optional) | Smoking Time: 4-6 hours
Resting Time: 15-30 min
Servings: 4-6

Ingredients:
For the Pork Ribs:

- 2 racks of pork ribs (baby back or St. Louis-style)
- Yellow mustard (for binding the rub)
- Wood chunks or chips for smoking (hickory, apple, or cherry work well)

For the BBQ Rub:

- 1/4 cup brown sugar
- 2 tablespoons paprika
- 1 tablespoon kosher salt
- 1 tablespoon black pepper
- 1 tablespoon garlic powder
- 1 tablespoon onion powder
- 1 teaspoon cayenne pepper (adjust to your preferred level of spiciness)

For the BBQ Sauce (optional):

- Your favorite BBQ sauce

Instructions:
Preparing the Pork Ribs:

1. Remove the Membrane: If your ribs still have the mem- brane on the bone side, carefully peel it off using a butter knife or a paper towel for better flavor penetration.

2. Marinating (Optional): Although marinating is optional, it can add extra flavor. You can rub the ribs with a bit of yellow mustard as a binder and then apply the BBQ rub. Allow the ribs to marinate in the refrigerator for 2-4 hours or overnight.

Preparing the BBQ Rub:

1. Mix the Rub: In a bowl, combine the brown sugar, paprika, kosher salt, black pepper, garlic powder, onion powder, and cayenne pepper. Mix well to create the BBQ rub.

2. Season the Ribs: Sprinkle and rub the BBQ rub evenly over both sides of the ribs, pressing it into the meat to create a flavorful crust. Be generous with the rub.

Smoking the Pork Ribs:

1. Preheat the Smoker: Preheat your smoker to a low and steady temperature of 225-250°F (107-121°C). Use wood chunks or chips for smoke flavor. Hickory, apple, or cherry wood are great choices.

2. Place the Ribs: Once the smoker is at the desired temper- ature, place the seasoned pork ribs on the smoker grates, bone side down. Insert a meat thermometer probe into one of the ribs to monitor the temperature.

3. Smoke Low and Slow: Smoke the ribs at a consistent temperature of 225-250°F (107-121°C) for 4-6 hours, depending on the thickness of the ribs and your preferred level of tenderness. The ribs are done when they reach an internal temperature of around 195-203°F (90-95°C) and have a nice bark on the outside.

4. Optional BBQ Sauce: If you prefer sauced ribs, you can baste the ribs with your favorite BBQ sauce during the last 30 minutes of smoking. This will give them a sticky and flavorful glaze.

Resting and Serving:

1. Rest the Ribs: Once the ribs are done, remove them from the smoker and let them rest for 15-30 minutes. This allows the juices to redistribute and keeps the ribs moist.

2. Slice and Serve: Slice the smoked pork ribs between the bones into individual portions. Serve them with additional BBQ sauce on the side if desired.

Enjoy your Smoked Pork Ribs, whether they're tender baby backs or flavorful St. Louis-style ribs, infused with that delicious smoky flavor!

Smoked Pork Belly

Preparation Time: 20 min | Marinating Time: 2-4 hours (optional) | Smoking Time: 3-4 hours

Resting Time: 15 min

Servings: 4-6

Ingredients:

For the Pork Belly:

- 2 pounds pork belly, skin removed
- Salt and black pepper, to taste
- Wood chunks or chips for smoking (apple, cherry, or oak) For the Marinade (optional):
- 1/4 cup soy sauce
- 1/4 cup brown sugar
- 2 tablespoons rice vinegar
- 2 cloves garlic, minced
- 1 tablespoon ginger, minced

Instructions:

Preparing the Pork Belly:

1. Remove the Skin: Start by removing the skin from the pork belly if it's still attached. A sharp knife can help you with this. You can ask your butcher to do this for you if needed.

2. Marinating (Optional): While marinating is optional, it can add extra flavor to the pork belly. In a bowl, mix together the soy sauce, brown sugar, rice vinegar, minced garlic, and minced ginger. Place the pork belly in a resealable plastic bag or a shallow dish and pour the marinade over it. Seal the bag or cover the dish and refrigerate for 2-4 hours or overnight.

Smoking the Pork Belly:

1. Preheat the Smoker: Preheat your smoker to a low and steady temperature of 225-250°F (107-121°C). Use wood chunks or chips for smoke flavor. Apple, cherry, or oak wood are great choices for pork belly.

2. Season the Pork Belly: Remove the marinated pork belly from the bag or dish and pat it dry with paper towels. Season it generously with salt and black pepper on all sides.

3. Place on the Smoker: Once the smoker is at the desired temperature, place the seasoned pork belly directly on the smoker grates, fat side up. Make sure to leave space between the slices if you're smoking multiple pieces.

4. Smoke Low and Slow: Smoke the pork belly at a con- sistent temperature of 225-250°F (107-121°C) for 3-4 hours. The pork belly is ready when it reaches an internal temperature of about 190-200°F (88-93°C) and the fat has rendered, making it tender and flavorful.

Resting and Serving:

1. Rest the Pork Belly: Remove the smoked pork belly from the smoker and let it rest for about 15 minutes. This allows the juices to redistribute and keeps the meat moist.

2. Slice and Serve: Slice the smoked pork belly into thin or thick pieces, depending on your preference. Serve it as a main dish or as a delicious addition to various recipes and dishes.

Enjoy your Smoked Pork Belly, featuring rich, tender meat and a delightful smoky flavor. It's a versatile ingredient that can be used in a variety of culinary creations!

Spicy Smoked Pork Carnitas

Preparation Time: 20 min | Smoking Time: 4-5 hours | Resting Time: 15 min
Servings: 6-8

Ingredients:
For the Smoked Pork:

- 4-5 pounds boneless pork shoulder (also known as pork butt)
- Wood chunks or chips for smoking (hickory or mesquite work well)

For the Rub:

- 2 tablespoons chili powder
- 1 tablespoon paprika
- 1 tablespoon cumin
- 1 tablespoon garlic powder
- 1 tablespoon onion powder
- 1 teaspoon cayenne pepper (adjust to your preferred level of spiciness)
- Salt and black pepper, to taste For the Crisping (Optional):
- 2 tablespoons vegetable oil

Instructions:
Preparing the Pork:

1. Preheat the Smoker: Preheat your smoker to a low and steady temperature of 225-250°F (107-121°C). Use wood chunks or chips for smoke flavor. Hickory or mesquite wood can add a bold smoky flavor.

2. Trim and Season the Pork: Trim excess fat from the pork shoulder, leaving some for flavor. In a small bowl, mix together the chili powder, paprika, cumin, garlic powder, onion powder, cayenne pepper, salt, and black pepper to create the rub. Rub the seasoning mixture evenly over the entire pork shoulder.

3. Place on the Smoker: Once the smoker is at the desired temperature, place the seasoned pork shoulder directly on the smoker grates.

4. Smoke Low and Slow: Smoke the pork shoulder at a consistent temperature of 225-250°F (107-121°C) for about 4-5 hours. The pork shoulder is ready when it reaches an internal temperature of around 195-203°F (90-95°C) and is tender enough to easily shred with a fork.

Resting and Shredding:

1. Rest the Smoked Pork: Remove the smoked pork shoul- der from the smoker and let it rest for about 15 minutes. This allows the juices to redistribute and keeps the meat moist.

2. Shred the Pork: Use two forks or your hands to shred the smoked pork into bite-sized pieces. You can also pull apart any larger chunks of meat. The more uneven and rustic, the better for carnitas.

Optional Crisping:

1. Crisp the Carnitas (Optional): For extra flavor and texture, you can crisp up the shredded pork carnitas. Heat 2 tablespoons of vegetable oil in a large skillet over medium-high heat. Add the shredded pork and cook for a few minutes, turning occasionally, until it's crispy on the edges.

Serving:

1. Serve: Serve the Spicy Smoked Pork Carnitas as tacos, burritos, or on a plate with your favorite toppings and sides, such as salsa, guacamole, diced onions, cilantro, and lime wedges.

Enjoy your Spicy Smoked Pork Carnitas, featuring tender, smoky, and boldly seasoned pork that's perfect for adding a spicy twist to your favorite Mexican dishes!

Smoker Recipes: Poultry

Applewood Smoked Whole Chicken

Preparation Time: 20 min | Brining Time: 4-6 hours (optional) | Smoking Time: 2.5-3.5 hours
Resting Time: 15 min
Servings: 4-6

Ingredients:
For the Whole Chicken:

- 1 whole chicken (about 4-5 pounds)
- Wood chunks or chips for smoking (applewood works perfectly)
- Salt and black pepper, to taste
- 2-3 tablespoons olive oil (for brushing) For the Brine (optional):
- 4 cups cold water
- 1/4 cup kosher salt
- 1/4 cup brown sugar
- 2 cloves garlic, minced
- 1 lemon, sliced
- 1 sprig fresh rosemary (or 1 tablespoon dried)
- 1 sprig fresh thyme (or 1 tablespoon dried)

Instructions:
Preparing the Whole Chicken:

1. Remove Giblets: If your chicken comes with giblets (neck, heart, liver), remove them and set them aside for other uses or discard them.

2. Brining (Optional): In a large container or brining bag, combine cold water, kosher salt, brown sugar, minced garlic, lemon slices, fresh rosemary, and fresh thyme. Stir until the salt and sugar are fully dissolved. Submerge the whole chicken in the brine, ensuring it's fully covered. Refrigerate for 4-6 hours. This step is optional but enhances flavor and tenderness.

3. Rinse and Pat Dry: After brining (or if you skip brining), remove the chicken from the brine, rinse it under cold water, and pat it dry with paper towels.

4. Season the Chicken: Season the chicken, inside and out, with salt and black pepper. Brush the exterior with olive oil for a crispy skin.

Smoking the Whole Chicken:

1. Preheat the Smoker: Preheat your smoker to a tempera- ture of 225-250°F (107-121°C). Use applewood chunks or chips for that delightful sweet and smoky flavor.

2. Prepare the Chicken: Place the seasoned and oiled chicken on the smoker grates, breast side up.

3. Smoke Low and Slow: Smoke the whole chicken at a consistent temperature of 225-250°F (107-121°C) for approximately 2.5-3.5 hours, or until the internal tem- perature reaches 165°F (74°C) in the thickest part of the thigh, avoiding touching the bone.

Resting and Serving:

1. Rest the Smoked Chicken: Remove the smoked whole chicken from the smoker and let it rest for about 15 minutes. This allows the juices to redistribute and keeps the meat moist.

2. Carve and Serve: Carve the smoked chicken into desired portions. Serve it with your favorite sides, such as roasted vegetables, coleslaw, or cornbread.

Enjoy your Applewood Smoked Whole Chicken, featuring a subtly sweet and smoky flavor that's sure to impress your family and guests at any gathering!

Hickory Smoked Chicken Wings

Preparation Time: 15 min | Smoking Time: 1.5-2 hours | Resting Time: 10 min
Servings: 4-6

Ingredients:
For the Chicken Wings:

- 2-3 pounds chicken wings, split into flats and drumettes
- Wood chunks or chips for smoking (hickory)
- 2 tablespoons vegetable oil (for brushing) For the Spicy Rub:
- 2 tablespoons paprika
- 1 tablespoon chili powder
- 1 tablespoon brown sugar
- 1 teaspoon garlic powder
- 1 teaspoon onion powder
- 1 teaspoon cayenne pepper (adjust to your preferred level of spiciness)
- 1 teaspoon salt
- 1/2 teaspoon black pepper

Instructions:
Preparing the Chicken Wings:

1. Rinse and Pat Dry: Rinse the chicken wings under cold water and pat them dry with paper towels. This helps the rub adhere better.

2. Season the Wings: In a bowl, mix together paprika, chili powder, brown sugar, garlic powder, onion powder, cayenne pepper, salt, and black pepper to create the spicy rub. Season the chicken wings generously with the rub, making sure to coat each wing evenly. You can do this in a large resealable bag for easy mixing.

Smoking the Chicken Wings:

1. Preheat the Smoker: Preheat your smoker to a tempera-ture of 225-250°F (107-121°C). Use hickory wood chunks or chips for a robust, smoky flavor.

2. Prepare the Chicken: Place the seasoned chicken wings on the smoker grates, leaving some space between each wing. Arrange them in a single layer, skin side up.

3. Smoke Low and Slow: Smoke the chicken wings at a consistent temperature of 225-250°F (107-121°C) for approximately 1.5-2 hours. The wings are ready when they reach an internal temperature of 165°F (74°C) and have a rich, smoky color and crispy skin.

Resting and Serving:

1. Rest the Smoked Wings: Remove the smoked chicken wings from the smoker and let them rest for about 10 minutes. This allows the juices to redistribute and keeps the meat tender.

2. Serve: Serve the Hickory Smoked Chicken Wings as an appetizer or main course with your favorite dipping sauces or sides, such as ranch dressing, blue cheese dip, celery sticks, and carrot sticks.

Enjoy your Hickory Smoked Chicken Wings with their rich, deep smoky flavor and spicy kick from the rub!

Lemon and Thyme Smoked Chicken Thighs

Preparation Time: 15 min | Marinating Time: 1-2 hours | Smoking Time: 1.5-2 hours

Resting Time: 10 min

Servings: 4-6

Ingredients:

For the Chicken Thighs:

- 8-10 bone-in, skin-on chicken thighs
- Wood chunks or chips for smoking (hickory or applewood work well)

For the Marinade:

- Zest and juice of 2 lemons
- 2 cloves garlic, minced
- 2 tablespoons fresh thyme leaves (or 2 teaspoons dried thyme)
- 2 tablespoons olive oil
- 1 teaspoon salt
- 1/2 teaspoon black pepper

Instructions:

Preparing the Chicken Thighs:

1. Marinate the Chicken: In a bowl, combine the lemon zest, lemon juice, minced garlic, fresh thyme leaves, olive oil, salt, and black pepper to create the marinade. Place the chicken thighs in a large resealable bag or a shallow dish and pour the marinade over them. Seal the bag or cover the dish and refrigerate for 1-2 hours to allow the flavors to infuse.

Smoking the Chicken Thighs:

1. Preheat the Smoker: Preheat your smoker to a tempera-ture of 225-250°F (107-121°C). Use wood chunks or chips for smoke flavor. Hickory or applewood can complement the lemon and thyme.

2. Prepare the Chicken: Remove the chicken thighs from the marinade and discard any excess marinade. Pat the thighs dry with paper towels.

3. Smoke Low and Slow: Once the smoker is ready, place the chicken thighs directly on the smoker grates, skin side up. Maintain a consistent temperature of 225-250°F (107-121°C) throughout the smoking process.

4. Smoke for Flavor: Smoke the chicken thighs for ap- proximately 1.5-2 hours or until they reach an internal temperature of 165°F (74°C) when measured with a meat thermometer. The thighs will have a beautiful smoky flavor and a crispy, golden skin.

Resting and Serving:

1. Rest the Smoked Chicken Thighs: Remove the smoked chicken thighs from the smoker and let them rest for about 10 minutes. This allows the juices to redistribute, ensuring tender and flavorful meat.

2. Serve: Serve the Lemon and Thyme Smoked Chicken Thighs as a main course with your favorite sides, such as grilled vegetables, rice, or a fresh garden salad. Garnish with additional fresh thyme leaves and lemon wedges if desired.

Enjoy your Lemon and Thyme Smoked Chicken Thighs, fea- turing a zesty and herby flavor that's perfect for any outdoor meal!

Spicy Smoked Chicken Drumsticks

Preparation Time: 15 min | Marinating Time: 1-2 hours (optional) | Smoking Time: 1.5-2 hours
Resting Time: 10 min
Servings: 4-6

Ingredients:
For the Chicken Drumsticks:

· 12-15 chicken drumsticks

· Wood chunks or chips for smoking (hickory or mesquite are excellent choices)

For the Spicy Rub:

· 2 tablespoons paprika

· 1 tablespoon chili powder

· 1 tablespoon brown sugar

· 1 teaspoon garlic powder

· 1 teaspoon onion powder

· 1 teaspoon cayenne pepper (adjust to your preferred level of spiciness)

· 1 teaspoon salt

· 1/2 teaspoon black pepper For the Optional Marinade:

· 1/4 cup buttermilk

· 1 tablespoon hot sauce (e.g., Tabasco)

Instructions:

Preparing the Chicken Drumsticks:

1. Optional Marinade: If you prefer, you can marinate the chicken drumsticks for added tenderness and flavor. In anbowl, combine the buttermilk and hot sauce. Submerge the drumsticks in this mixture, cover, and refrigerate for 1-2 hours. This step is optional but recommended.

2. Prepare the Drumsticks: Remove the drumsticks from the marinade (if used) and pat them dry with paper towels.

3. Season with Spicy Rub: In a bowl, mix together the paprika, chili powder, brown sugar, garlic powder, onion powder, cayenne pepper, salt, and black pepper to create the spicy rub. Generously coat each drumstick with the rub, ensuring they are well-covered.

Smoking the Chicken Drumsticks:

1. Preheat the Smoker: Preheat your smoker to a tem- perature of 225-250°F (107-121°C). Use wood chunks or chips for smoke flavor. Hickory or mesquite wood pairs wonderfully with the spicy rub.

2. Place on the Smoker: Arrange the seasoned chicken drumsticks on the smoker grates, leaving some space between them to allow for even smoking.

3. Smoke Low and Slow: Smoke the drumsticks at a con- sistent temperature of 225-250°F (107-121°C) for ap- proximately 1.5-2 hours. The drumsticks are ready when they reach an internal temperature of 165°F (74°C) when measured with a meat thermometer. They will have a delightful smoky flavor and crispy skin.

Resting and Serving:

1. Rest the Smoked Drumsticks: Remove the smoked chicken drumsticks from the smoker and let them rest for about 10 minutes. This allows the juices to redis- tribute and keeps the meat moist and tender.

2. Serve: Serve the Spicy Smoked Chicken Drumsticks as a delightful finger food or alongside your favorite sides, such as coleslaw, potato salad, or cornbread. Provide extra hot sauce or dipping sauces for those who crave an extra kick.

Enjoy your Spicy Smoked Chicken Drumsticks, featuring a spicy and smoky flavor that's perfect for any gathering or barbecue!

Smoked Turkey Breast with Herb Rub

Preparation Time: 20 min | Brining Time: 12-24 hours (optional) | Smoking Time: 3-4 hours
Resting Time: 20-30 min
Servings: 6-8

Ingredients:

For the Turkey Breast:

- 1 bone-in turkey breast (about 5-6 pounds)
- Wood chunks or chips for smoking (fruitwoods like apple or cherry work well)
- 1-2 tablespoons vegetable oil (for brushing) For the Herb Rub:
- 2 tablespoons dried rosemary
- 2 tablespoons dried thyme
- 2 tablespoons dried sage
- 1 tablespoon dried oregano
- 1 tablespoon garlic powder
- 1 tablespoon onion powder
- 1 tablespoon kosher salt
- 1/2 tablespoon black pepper
- 1/4 cup olive oil (for mixing into the rub) For the Optional Brine:
- 4 cups cold water
- 1/4 cup kosher salt
- 1/4 cup brown sugar
- 2 cloves garlic, minced
- 1 lemon, sliced
- 1 sprig fresh rosemary
- 1 sprig fresh thyme

Instructions:

Preparing the Turkey Breast:

1. Optional Brining (Recommended): In a large container or brining bag, combine cold water, kosher salt, brown sugar, minced garlic, lemon slices, fresh rosemary, and fresh thyme. Stir until the salt and sugar dissolve. Submerge the turkey

breast in the brine, ensuring it's fully covered. Refrigerate for 12-24 hours. This step is optional but enhances flavor and moisture.

2. Remove from Brine: If you've brined the turkey breast, remove it from the brine, rinse it under cold water, and pat it dry with paper towels. If not, simply rinse and pat dry.

3. Prepare the Herb Rub: In a bowl, combine the dried rosemary, dried thyme, dried sage, dried oregano, garlic powder, onion powder, kosher salt, black pepper, and olive oil. Mix until you have a paste-like consistency.

4. Rub the Turkey: Carefully separate the skin from the turkey breast by gently sliding your fingers underneath it. Rub the herb mixture directly onto the meat, under the skin, and on the skin's surface. Ensure an even coating.

Smoking the Turkey Breast:

1. Preheat the Smoker: Preheat your smoker to a tempera- ture of 225-250°F (107-121°C). Use wood chunks or chips for smoke flavor. Fruitwoods like apple or cherry are ideal for turkey.

2. Prepare the Turkey for Smoking: Brush the outside of the turkey breast with vegetable oil. This will help the skin become crisp and golden during smoking.

3. Smoke Low and Slow: Place the prepared turkey breast on the smoker grates, skin side up. Insert a meat thermometer probe into the thickest part of the breast.

4. Maintain the Temperature: Smoke the turkey breast at a consistent temperature of 225-250°F (107-121°C) for approximately 3-4 hours or until the internal temperature reaches 165°F (74°C). The turkey will have a beautiful smoky flavor and a crisp, golden skin.

Resting and Serving:

1. Rest the Smoked Turkey Breast: Remove the smoked turkey breast from the smoker and let it rest for 20-30 minutes. This allows the juices to redistribute and keeps the meat tender.

2. Carve and Serve: Carve the smoked turkey breast into slices and serve it as a delightful main course. It pairs wonder-fully with your favorite sides, such as stuffing, roasted vegetables, or cranberry sauce.

Enjoy your Smoked Turkey Breast with Herb Rub, featuring a deliciously aromatic and smoky flavor that's perfect for any festive occasion!

Maple-Bourbon Smoked Turkey

Preparation Time: 24-48 hours (including brining) | Brining Time: 12-24 hours | Smoking Time: 4-6 hours

Resting Time: 30-45 min

Servings: 10-12

Ingredients:

For the Turkey:

- 12-14-pound whole turkey, thawed and giblets removed
- Wood chunks or chips for smoking (hickory or applewood work well)

For the Brine:

- 1 gallon cold water
- 1 cup kosher salt
- 1 cup brown sugar
- 1 cup pure maple syrup
- 1 cup bourbon whiskey
- 2 oranges, sliced
- 2 lemons, sliced
- 4 sprigs fresh rosemary
- 4 sprigs fresh thyme
- 4 cloves garlic, smashed For the Rub:
- 1/4 cup softened unsalted butter
- 2 tablespoons pure maple syrup
- 1 tablespoon bourbon whiskey
- 1 teaspoon dried thyme
- 1 teaspoon dried sage
- 1 teaspoon salt
- 1/2 teaspoon black pepper

Instructions:

Brining the Turkey:

1. Prepare the Brine: In a large stockpot or container, combine cold water, kosher salt, brown sugar, pure maple syrup, bourbon whiskey, sliced oranges, sliced lemons, fresh rosemary, fresh thyme, and smashed garlic. Stir until the salt and sugar are dissolved.

2. Submerge the Turkey: Place the whole turkey into the brine, ensuring it's fully submerged. If necessary, weigh the turkey down with a plate or heavy object to keep it submerged. Cover and refrigerate for 12-24 hours, allowing the turkey to absorb the flavorful brine.

Preparing and Smoking the Turkey:

1. Remove and Rinse: After the brining period, remove the turkey from the brine and rinse it under cold water. Pat it dry with paper towels.

2. Prepare the Rub: In a bowl, mix together the softened unsalted butter, pure maple syrup, bourbon whiskey, dried thyme, dried sage, salt, and black pepper to create the rub.

3. Rub the Turkey: Carefully separate the skin from the turkey by gently sliding your fingers underneath it. Rub the prepared butter and maple-bourbon mixture under the skin, directly onto the meat. Then, rub any remaining mixture over the skin's surface.

4. Preheat the Smoker: Preheat your smoker to a tem- perature of 225-250°F (107-121°C). Use wood chunks or chips for a smoky flavor. Hickory or applewood are great choices for poultry.

5. Smoke the Turkey: Place the prepared turkey onto the smoker grates, breast side up. Insert a meat thermome- ter probe into the thickest part of the breast.

6. Maintain the Temperature: Smoke the turkey at a consistent temperature of 225-250°F (107-121°C) for ap- proximately 4-6 hours or until the internal temperature reaches 165°F (74°C). Baste the turkey with any drippings or leftover rub mixture every hour to keep it moist and flavorful.

Resting and Serving:

1. Rest the Smoked Turkey: Remove the smoked turkey from the smoker and let it rest, tented with aluminum foil, for 30-45 minutes. This resting period allows the juices to redistribute, ensuring a juicy and flavorful turkey.

2. Carve and Serve: Carve the Maple-Bourbon Smoked Turkey into slices and serve it as the centerpiece of your holiday feast. Accompany it with your favorite side dishes, such as mashed potatoes, green beans, and cranberry sauce.

Enjoy your Maple-Bourbon Smoked Turkey, featuring a har- monious blend of sweet and smoky flavors that will delight your family and guests on any special occasion!

Smoked Turkey Legs

Preparation Time: 20 min | Brining Time: 4-6 hours (optional) | Smoking Time: 3-4 hours

Resting Time: 10 min

Servings: 4

Ingredients:

For the Turkey Legs:

- 4 large turkey legs
- Wood chunks or chips for smoking (hickory or mesquite work well)

For the BBQ Rub:

- 2 tablespoons brown sugar
- 1 tablespoon paprika
- 1 teaspoon garlic powder
- 1 teaspoon onion powder
- 1 teaspoon chili powder
- 1 teaspoon black pepper
- 1 teaspoon salt
- 1/2 teaspoon cayenne pepper (adjust to your preferred level of spiciness)

For the Optional Brine:

- 4 cups cold water
- 1/4 cup kosher salt
- 1/4 cup brown sugar
- 2 cloves garlic, minced
- 1 tablespoon black peppercorns
- 1 bay leaf

Instructions:

Preparing the Turkey Legs:

1. Optional Brining (Recommended): In a large container or brining bag, combine cold water, kosher salt, brown sugar, minced garlic, black peppercorns, and a bay leaf. Stir until the salt and sugar dissolve. Submerge the turkey legs in the brine, ensuring they are fully covered. Refrigerate for 4-6 hours. This step is optional but enhances flavor and moisture.

2. Remove from Brine: If you've brined the turkey legs, remove them from the brine, rinse them under cold water, and pat them dry with paper towels. If not, simply rinse and pat dry.

3. Prepare the BBQ Rub: In a bowl, mix together the brown sugar, paprika, garlic powder, onion powder, chili powder, black pepper, salt, and cayenne pepper to create the BBQ rub.

4. Rub the Turkey Legs: Generously coat each turkey leg with the BBQ rub, ensuring they are well-covered. Press the rub onto the meat to adhere.

Smoking the Turkey Legs:

1. Preheat the Smoker: Preheat your smoker to a tem- perature of 225-250°F (107-121°C). Use wood chunks or chips for smoke flavor. Hickory or mesquite wood pairs wonderfully with turkey legs.

2. Place on the Smoker: Arrange the seasoned turkey legs on the smoker grates.

3. Smoke Low and Slow: Smoke the turkey legs at a consistent temperature of 225-250°F (107-121°C) for approximately 3-4 hours or until they reach an internal temperature of 165°F (74°C) when measured with a meat thermometer. The turkey legs will have a smoky, crispy skin and tender meat.

Resting and Serving:

1. 1Rest the Smoked Turkey Legs: Remove the smoked turkey legs from the smoker and let them rest for about 10 minutes. This allows the juices to redistribute and keeps the meat moist and tender.

2. Serve: Serve the Smoked Turkey Legs as a fun and fla- vorful main course. Enjoy them at picnics, barbecues, or as a tasty treat reminiscent of fairground-style smoked legs.

These Smoked Turkey Legs are a delightful and savory treat that will transport you to the fairground experience right at home!

Smoker Recipes: Seafood

Applewood Smoked Salmon

Preparation Time: 15 min | Brining Time: 1-2 hours (optional) | Smoking Time: 1-2 hours
Resting Time: 20-30 min
Servings: 4

Ingredients:
For the Salmon:

- 4 salmon fillets (skin-on or skinless, about 6-8 ounces each)
- Applewood chunks or chips for smoking For the Brine (Optional):
- 4 cups cold water
- 1/4 cup kosher salt
- 1/4 cup brown sugar
- 2 cloves garlic, minced
- 1 lemon, sliced
- 1 sprig fresh dill
- 1 sprig fresh thyme

For the Dry Rub:

- 2 tablespoons brown sugar
- 1 teaspoon black pepper
- 1 teaspoon paprika
- 1/2 teaspoon garlic powder
- 1/2 teaspoon onion powder
- 1/2 teaspoon dried dill
- 1/2 teaspoon dried thyme
- 1/4 teaspoon cayenne pepper (optional, for heat)

Instructions:

Preparing the Salmon:

1. Optional Brining (Recommended): In a large container or brining bag, combine cold water, kosher salt, brown sugar, minced garlic, lemon slices, fresh dill, and fresh thyme. Stir until the salt and sugar dissolve. Submerge the salmon fillets in the brine, cover, and refrigerate for 1-2 hours. This step is optional but enhances flavor and moisture.

2. Remove from Brine: After the brining period, remove the salmon fillets from the brine, rinse them under cold water, and pat them dry with paper towels. If not brining, simply rinse and pat dry.

3. Prepare the Dry Rub: In a bowl, mix together the brown sugar, black pepper, paprika, garlic powder, onion pow- der, dried dill, dried thyme, and cayenne pepper (if using) to create the dry rub.

4. Rub the Salmon: Sprinkle the dry rub evenly over the salmon fillets, ensuring they are well-coated on all sides. Press the rub onto the salmon to adhere.

Smoking the Salmon:

1. Preheat the Smoker: Preheat your smoker to a temper- ature of 180-200°F (82-93°C). Use applewood chunks or chips for smoke flavor. Applewood imparts a subtle, sweet smokiness that complements salmon beautifully.

2. Place on the Smoker: Arrange the seasoned salmon fillets on the smoker grates, skin-side down if they have skin.

3. Smoke Low and Slow: Smoke the salmon at a consistent temperature of 180-200°F (82-93°C) for approximately 1-2 hours or until the internal temperature reaches 145°F (63°C) when measured with a meat thermometer. The salmon will have a beautiful smoky flavor, a flaky texture, and a delicious crust.

Resting and Serving:

1. Rest the Smoked Salmon: Remove the smoked salmon from the smoker and let it rest for about 20-30 minutes. This allows the juices to redistribute and keeps the fish moist and flavorful.

2. Serve: Serve the Applewood Smoked Salmon as a delight- ful main course. It pairs wonderfully with a fresh green salad, creamy dill sauce, or lemon wedges for added zing.

Enjoy your Applewood Smoked Salmon, featuring a delicate sweetness from the applewood smoke that beautifully com- ple- ments the richness of the salmon!

Smoked Trout with Dill and Lemon

Preparation Time: 15 min | Smoking Time: 1-2 hours | Resting Time: 15 min
Servings: 4

Ingredients:

- 4 whole trout, gutted and cleaned
- Wood chips for smoking (preferably fruitwood like apple or cherry)

For the Dill and Lemon Seasoning:

- 2 tablespoons fresh dill, chopped
- Zest of 1 lemon
- Juice of 1 lemon
- 2 cloves garlic, minced
- 2 tablespoons olive oil
- Salt and black pepper to taste

Instructions:

Preparing the Trout:

1. Prepare the Dill and Lemon Seasoning: In a bowl, combine the chopped fresh dill, lemon zest, lemon juice, minced garlic, olive oil, salt, and black pepper. Mix well to create the seasoning mixture.
2. Season the Trout: Gently rub the seasoning mixture inside and outside each trout, ensuring they are well-coated with the dill and lemon flavor. Allow the trout to marinate in the seasoning for about 15 minutes while you prepare the smoker.

Smoking the Trout:

1. Preheat the Smoker: Preheat your smoker to a tempera-ture of 180-200°F (82-93°C). Use wood chips for smoking, preferably fruitwood like apple or cherry, to impart a mild and delicate smoky flavor that complements the trout.
2. Place on the Smoker: Arrange the seasoned trout on the smoker grates, leaving space between each fish for the smoke to circulate.
3. Smoke Low and Slow: Smoke the trout at a consistent temperature of 180-200°F (82-93°C) for approximately 1-2 hours, or until the flesh flakes easily with a fork. The delicate smoke will infuse the trout with a subtle, herby flavor.

Resting and Serving:

1. Rest the Smoked Trout: Remove the smoked trout from the smoker and let them rest for about 15 minutes. This allows the flavors to meld and the juices to redistribute, resulting in a tender and flavorful dish.

2. Serve: Serve the Smoked Trout with Dill and Lemon as an elegant and delicious main course. Garnish with addi- tional fresh dill and lemon wedges for extra brightness and flavor.

Enjoy your Smoked Trout with Dill and Lemon, a dish that showcases the delicate flavors of trout enhanced by the refreshing combination of dill and lemon, all subtly comple- mented by the gentle smokiness!

For the Smoked Mackerel:

- 4 whole mackerel, gutted and cleaned
- Wood chips for smoking (cedar or alder work well)
- Olive oil for brushing
- Salt and black pepper to taste For the Horseradish Cream:
- 1/2 cup sour cream
- 2 tablespoons prepared horseradish (adjust to taste)
- 1 tablespoon lemon juice
- 1 teaspoon Dijon mustard
- 1 teaspoon honey
- 1 clove garlic, minced
- Salt and black pepper to taste
- Fresh chives, chopped (for garnish)

Instructions:
Preparing the Smoked Mackerel:

1. Preheat the Smoker: Preheat your smoker to a tem- perature of 180-200°F (82-93°C). Use wood chips for smoking, such as cedar or alder, which pair nicely withmackerel.

2. Brush with Olive Oil: Brush the whole mackerel on both sides with olive oil. This will help the fish achieve a beautiful golden color during smoking.

3. Season with Salt and Pepper: Season the mackerel generously with salt and black pepper, both inside and outside the fish.

4. Place on the Smoker: Arrange the seasoned mackerel on the smoker grates, making sure there is enough space betwe- en them for the smoke to circulate evenly.

5. Smoke Low and Slow: Smoke the mackerel at a consis- tent temperature of 180-200°F (82-93°C) for approx- imately 2-3 hours, or until the flesh is flaky and has absorbed the wonderful smoky flavor. Keep an eye on the fish to avoid overcooking.

Preparing the Horseradish Cream:

1. Make the Horseradish Cream: In a bowl, combine the sour cream, prepared horseradish (adjust to your preferred level of spiciness), lemon juice, Dijon mustard, honey, minced garlic, salt, and black pepper. Mix well until all the ingredients are fully incorporated. Taste and adjust the seasoning if needed.

Serving:

1. Serve with Horseradish Cream: Once the smoked mack- erel is ready, serve it with a dollop of the prepared Horsera- dish Cream on the side. Garnish with chopped fresh chives for a pop of color and additional flavor.

2. Enjoy: Smoked Mackerel with Horseradish Cream makes for an excellent appetizer or light meal. The smokiness of the mackerel pairs beautifully with the tangy and spicy horseradish cream.

This dish offers a harmonious balance of flavors and textures, making it a delightful choice for any seafood enthusiast or anyone looking to savor a delicious smoked fish appetizer.

Cedar Plank Smoked Cod

Preparation Time: 15 min | Smoking Time: 25-30 min

Servings: 4

Ingredients:

- 4 cod fillets (about 6-8 ounces each)
- 1 cedar plank (soaked in water for at least 1 hour)
- Olive oil for brushing
- Salt and black pepper to taste
- Fresh lemon wedges (for serving)
- Fresh parsley, chopped (for garnish)

Instructions:

Preparing the Cedar Plank:

1. Soak the Cedar Plank: Place the cedar plank in a large container or sink filled with water. Allow it to soak for at least 1 hour. This soaking process will prevent the plank from burning during the smoking process and infuse the cod with a pleasant woody flavor.

Preparing the Cod:

1. Preheat the Smoker: Preheat your smoker to a tempera- ture of 225-250°F (107-121°C). Use wood chips or chunks of your choice for smoking. Fruitwoods like apple or cherry work well with cod.

2. Season the Cod: Pat the cod fillets dry with paper towels. Brush both sides of each fillet with olive oil. Season with salt and black pepper to taste. This simple seasoning allows the natural flavor of the cod to shine through.

Smoking the Cod:

1. Place the Cedar Plank on the Grill Grates: Once the cedar plank has soaked and the smoker is at the desired tempe- rature, place the wet cedar plank directly on the grill grates. Allow it to heat for a few minutes until it starts to produce a bit of smoke and becomes fragrant.

2. Place the Cod on the Plank: Carefully place the seasoned cod fillets, skin-side down, onto the heated cedar plank.

3. Smoke Low and Slow: Close the smoker lid and smoke the cod at a consistent temperature of 225-250°F (107-121°C) for about 25-30 minutes or until the fish flakes easily with a fork. The cedar plank will impart a distinct smoky, woody aroma and flavor to the cod.

Serving:

1. Serve Immediately: Carefully remove the cedar plank with the smoked cod from the smoker. Serve the smoked cod fillets on the cedar plank itself for a rustic presenta- tion.

2. Garnish and Enjoy: Garnish the smoked cod with fresh lemon wedges and chopped fresh parsley for a burst of flavor and color. Serve immediately while it's hot and aromatic.

Cedar Plank Smoked Cod is a delightful dish that showcases the natural flavors of cod enhanced by the subtle woody notes from the cedar plank. It's perfect for seafood enthusiasts and those who appreciate the unique taste of smoked fish.

Asian-Inspired Smoked Halibut

Preparation Time: 20 min | Marinating Time: 30 min | Smoking Time: 30-40 min
Servings: 4

Ingredients:
For the Halibut and Marinade:

- 4 halibut fillets (6-8 ounces each)
- 1/4 cup soy sauce
- 2 tablespoons sesame oil
- 2 tablespoons rice vinegar
- 2 tablespoons fresh ginger, minced
- 2 cloves garlic, minced
- 2 tablespoons honey
- 1 tablespoon sesame seeds (optional)
- Salt and black pepper to taste For Smoking:
- Wood chips or chunks for smoking (fruitwood like apple or cherry works well)

For Garnish:

- Fresh cilantro leaves
- Sliced green onions
- Lime wedges

Instructions:
Preparing the Marinade:

1. Prepare the Marinade: In a bowl, combine soy sauce, sesame oil, rice vinegar, minced fresh ginger, minced garlic, honey, sesame seeds (if using), salt, and black pepper. Whisk the ingredients together to create the Asian-inspired marinade.

Marinating the Halibut:

1. Marinate the Halibut: Place the halibut fillets in a shallow dish or resealable plastic bag. Pour the marinade over the halibut, ensuring that all sides are coated. Seal the bag or cover the dish and refrigerate for 30 minutes to allow the halibut to absorb the flavors.

Preparing the Smoker:

1. Preheat the Smoker: Preheat your smoker to a tem- perature of 225-250°F (107-121°C) using wood chips or chunks (fruitwood like apple or cherry) for a mild and sweet smoky flavor.

Smoking the Halibut:

1. Prepare the Halibut for Smoking: Remove the mar- inated halibut fillets from the dish or bag and allow any excess marinade to drip off. You can reserve some marinade for basting during smoking.

2. Place on the Smoker: Place the halibut fillets directly on the smoker grates, ensuring they are well-spaced for even smoking.

3. Smoke Low and Slow: Smoke the halibut fillets at a consistent temperature of 225-250°F (107-121°C) for approximately 30-40 minutes, or until they are opaque and flake easily with a fork. Baste the fillets with the reserved marinade during smoking for an extra burst of flavor.

Serving:

1. Serve Hot: Carefully remove the smoked halibut fillets from the smoker.

2. Garnish and Enjoy: Garnish with fresh cilantro leaves, sliced green onions, and lime wedges. Serve the Asian-Inspired Smoked Halibut hot.

This Asian-Inspired Smoked Halibut is a delightful fusion of flavors, with the smokiness complementing the soy, ginger, and sesame marinade beautifully. It's an elegant dish that's perfect for a special dinner or any seafood lover's palate. Enjoy!

Hickory Smoked Shrimp with Cajun Spice

Preparation Time: 15 min | Marinating Time: 30 min | Smoking Time: 20-25 min
Servings: 4

Ingredients:
For the Smoked Shrimp:

- 1 pound large shrimp, peeled and deveined
- Wood chips (hickory) for smoking
- Olive oil for brushing For the Cajun Spice Mix:
- 1 tablespoon paprika
- 1 teaspoon garlic powder
- 1 teaspoon onion powder
- 1 teaspoon dried thyme
- 1/2 teaspoon dried oregano
- 1/2 teaspoon cayenne pepper (adjust to taste)
- 1/2 teaspoon black pepper
- 1/2 teaspoon white pepper
- 1/2 teaspoon salt
- 1/4 teaspoon smoked paprika (optional, for extra smoki- ness)

For Serving:

- Lemon wedges
- Fresh parsley, chopped (for garnish)

Instructions:
Preparing the Cajun Spice Mix:

1. Prepare the Cajun Spice Mix: In a small bowl, combine paprika, garlic powder, onion powder, dried thyme, dried oregano, cayenne pepper, black pepper, white pepper, salt, and smoked paprika (if using). Mix well to create the Cajun spice mix.

Marinating the Shrimp:

1. Marinate the Shrimp: In a large bowl, toss the peeled and deveined shrimp with the Cajun spice mix. Ensure that the shrimp are evenly coated with the spices. Cover the bowl and let the shrimp marinate in the refrigerator for about 30 minutes to allow the flavors to meld.

Preparing the Smoker:

1. Preheat the Smoker: Preheat your smoker to a tempera- ture of 225-250°F (107-121°C) using hickory wood chips for a robust smoky flavor.

Smoking the Shrimp:

1. Skewer the Shrimp: Thread the marinated shrimp onto skewers, ensuring they are spaced evenly to allow for even smoking.

2. Brush with Olive Oil: Lightly brush the shrimp with olive oil. This helps them develop a beautiful color during smoking.

3. Smoke Low and Slow: Place the shrimp skewers directly on the smoker grates. Smoke the shrimp at a consistent temperature of 225-250°F (107-121°C) for about 20-25 minutes or until they are pink and opaque, with a slight char from the smoke.

Serving:

1. Serve Hot: Carefully remove the smoked shrimp skewers from the smoker.

2. Garnish and Enjoy: Serve the Hickory Smoked Shrimp with Cajun Spice hot with lemon wedges and a sprinkle of fresh chopped parsley for a pop of color and freshness.

These smoked shrimp are bursting with flavor, with the Cajun spice mix adding a delightful kick. The hickory smoke infuses a deep, robust smokiness that pairs perfectly with the shrimp's natural sweetness. Enjoy as an appetizer or as part of a seafood feast!

Smoked Lobster Tails with Garlic Butter

Preparation Time: 15 min | Smoking Time: 20-25 min

Servings: 4

Ingredients:

For the Smoked Lobster Tails:

- 4 lobster tails, shell-on
- Olive oil for brushing
- Wood chips (fruitwood like apple or cherry) for smoking For the Garlic Butter Sauce:
- 1/2 cup (1 stick) unsalted butter
- 4 cloves garlic, minced
- 1 tablespoon fresh lemon juice
- 1 tablespoon fresh parsley, chopped
- Salt and black pepper to taste
- Lemon wedges (for serving)
- Fresh parsley, chopped (for garnish)

Instructions:

Preparing the Smoked Lobster Tails:

1. Preheat the Smoker: Preheat your smoker to a tem- perature of 225-250°F (107-121°C). Use wood chips, prefera- bly fruitwood like apple or cherry, for a delicate and sweet smoky flavor.

2. Prepare the Lobster Tails: Using kitchen shears, care- fully cut the top of each lobster tail down the center, stopping at the tail fan. Be sure not to cut through the bottom shell. Gently pry the shells apart to create a space for the garlic butter later.

3. Brush with Olive Oil: Brush the exposed lobster meat with olive oil to keep it moist during smoking.

Smoking the Lobster Tails:

1. Place on the Smoker: Arrange the prepared lobster tails directly on the smoker grates, meat-side up, ensuring they are well-spaced for even smoking.

2. Smoke Low and Slow: Smoke the lobster tails at a consistent temperature of 225-250°F (107-121°C) for approxi- mately 20-25 minutes, or until the lobster meat is opaque and the shells have turned a vibrant red color. The delicate smoky flavor will complement the lobster beautifully.

Preparing the Garlic Butter Sauce:

1. Make the Garlic Butter Sauce: While the lobster tails are smoking, prepare the garlic butter sauce. In a saucepan over medium heat, melt the unsalted butter. Add the minced garlic and sauté for about 1-2 minutes, or until fragrant.

2. Add Lemon and Parsley: Stir in the fresh lemon juice and chopped parsley. Season with salt and black pepper to taste. Allow the sauce to simmer for another minute or two. Remove from heat.

Serving:

1. Serve Hot: Carefully remove the smoked lobster tails from the smoker.

2. Serve with Garlic Butter: Drizzle the warm garlic butter sauce over the smoked lobster tails. Garnish with fresh chopped parsley and serve with lemon wedges on the side.

Smoked Lobster Tails with Garlic Butter is an exquisite dish that combines the delicate sweetness of lobster with the rich and savory garlic butter sauce. It's perfect for a special occasion or a luxurious seafood feast. Enjoy!

Smoked Oysters with Chili-Lime Dressing

Preparation Time: 15 min | Smoking Time: 20-30 min

Servings: 4

Ingredients:

For the Smoked Oysters:

- 24 fresh oysters, in their shells
- Wood chips for smoking (fruitwood like apple or cherry works well)

For the Chili-Lime Dressing:

- Juice of 2 limes
- Zest of 1 lime
- 1-2 red chili peppers, finely chopped (adjust to taste)
- 2 cloves garlic, minced
- 2 tablespoons fresh cilantro, chopped
- 1 tablespoon olive oil
- Salt and black pepper to taste For Garnish:
- Fresh cilantro leaves
- Lime wedges

Instructions:

Preparing the Smoked Oysters:

1. Preheat the Smoker: Preheat your smoker to a temper- ature of 225-250°F (107-121°C) using fruitwood chips like apple or cherry for a delicate smoky flavor.
2. Shucking the Oysters: Carefully shuck the fresh oysters, keeping them in their half shells. Discard the top shell, leaving the oysters nestled in the bottom shell.
3. Arrange on a Tray: Arrange the shucked oysters on a tray, ensuring they are well-spaced for even smoking.

Smoking the Oysters:

1. Place on the Smoker: Place the tray with the shucked oysters directly on the smoker grates. Smoke the oysters at a

consistent temperature of 225-250°F (107-121°C) for approximately 20-30 minutes, or until they take on a subtle smoky flavor.

Preparing the Chili-Lime Dressing:

1. Make the Chili-Lime Dressing: In a bowl, combine the juice of 2 limes, lime zest, finely chopped red chili peppers (adjust the amount to your preferred level of spiciness), minced garlic, fresh chopped cilantro, olive oil, salt, and black pepper. Mix well to create the zesty chili-lime dressing.

Serving:

1. Serve Hot: Carefully remove the smoked oysters from the smoker.
2. Drizzle with Chili-Lime Dressing: Drizzle the prepared chili-lime dressing over the smoked oysters while they are still warm.
3. Garnish and Enjoy: Garnish with fresh cilantro leaves and serve with lime wedges on the side. Serve immedi- ately.

Smoked Oysters with Chili-Lime Dressing is a delightful appetizer that offers a perfect balance of smokiness and zesty flavors. The subtle smoky notes of the oysters are complemented beautifully by the vibrant and tangy dressing. Enjoy this dish as a starter for a special occasion or as a unique addition to your seafood repertoire!

Maple-Glazed Smoked Scallops

Preparation Time: 20 min | Brining Time: 30 min | Smoking Time: 20-30 min
Servings: 4

Ingredients:

For the Maple Brine:

- 1/4 cup maple syrup
- 1/4 cup water
- 2 tablespoons salt
- 1 tablespoon brown sugar
- 1/2 teaspoon black pepper
- 1/2 teaspoon garlic powder
- 1/2 teaspoon onion powder For the Scallops:
- 1 pound fresh scallops
- Olive oil for brushing
- Maple glaze (see below)

For the Maple Glaze:

- 1/4 cup maple syrup
- 2 tablespoons melted butter
- 1 tablespoon Dijon mustard
- /2 teaspoon smoked paprika
- Salt and black pepper to taste

Instructions:

Preparing the Maple Brine:

1. Prepare the Maple Brine: In a bowl, combine maple syrup, water, salt, brown sugar, black pepper, garlic powder, and onion powder. Stir until the salt and sugar are fully dissolved to create the maple brine.

2. Brine the Scallops: Place the fresh scallops in a reseal- able plastic bag or a shallow dish. Pour the maple brine over the scallops, ensuring they are fully submerged. Seal the bag or cover the dish and refrigerate for 30 minutes to allow the scallops to absorb the flavors.

Preparing the Maple Glaze:

1. Make the Maple Glaze: In a separate bowl, whisk together maple syrup, melted butter, Dijon mustard, smoked paprika, salt, and black pepper. This will be used as a glaze for the scallops during smoking.

Smoking the Scallops:

1. Preheat the Smoker: Preheat your smoker to a tem- perature of 225-250°F (107-121°C) using wood chips or chunks for smoking (fruitwood like apple or cherry works well).

2. Prepare the Scallops: Remove the scallops from the maple brine and pat them dry with paper towels. Brush the scallops lightly with olive oil to prevent sticking during smoking.

3. Smoke Low and Slow: Place the prepared scallops directly on the smoker grates. Smoke the scallops at a consistent temperature of 225-250°F (107-121°C) for about 20-30 minutes, or until they are opaque and have a light smoky flavor.

4. Brush with Maple Glaze: During the last 5-10 minutes of smoking, brush the scallops generously with the maple glaze. This will caramelize and add a sweet, smoky layer of flavor.

Serving:

1. Serve Hot: Carefully remove the smoked scallops from the smoker.

2. Serve with Maple Glaze: Drizzle any remaining maple glaze over the smoked scallops.

3. Enjoy: Maple-Glazed Smoked Scallops are best enjoyed hot off the smoker. Serve them as an appetizer or as part of a seafood feast.

These Maple-Glazed Smoked Scallops are a perfect blend of sweet and smoky flavors, making them an elegant and irresistible dish. They're sure to impress your guests at any gathering or special occasion. Enjoy!

Smoked Clams with Garlic and Herbs

Preparation Time: 15 min | Smoking Time: 15-20 min
Servings: 4

Ingredients:
For the Clams:

- 24 fresh clams (littlenecks or cherrystones), scrubbed and cleaned
- Olive oil for brushing For the Garlic and Herb Mix:
- 4 cloves garlic, minced
- 2 tablespoons fresh parsley, chopped
- 2 tablespoons fresh cilantro, chopped
- 1 tablespoon fresh thyme leaves
- 1/4 cup unsalted butter, melted
- Zest and juice of 1 lemon
- Salt and black pepper to taste

Instructions:
Preparing the Clams:

1. Preheat the Smoker: Preheat your smoker to a tem- perature of 225-250°F (107-121°C) using wood chips or chunks (fruitwood like apple or cherry) for a mild smoky flavor.
2. Scrub and Clean the Clams: Scrub the fresh clams under cold running water to remove any dirt or debris. Discard any clams with open shells that don't close when tapped. Place the cleaned clams on a tray.

Preparing the Garlic and Herb Mix:

1. Make the Garlic and Herb Mix: In a bowl, combine minced garlic, fresh chopped parsley, fresh chopped cilantro, fresh thyme leaves, melted unsalted butter, lemon zest, and lemon juice. Season with salt and black pepper to taste. Mix well to create the garlic and herb mixture.

Smoking the Clams:

1. Brush with Olive Oil: Brush the cleaned clams lightly with olive oil to prevent sticking during smoking.

2. Place on the Smoker: Arrange the prepared clams di- rectly on the smoker grates, ensuring they are well- spaced for even smoking.

3. Smoke Low and Slow: Smoke the clams at a consis- tent temperature of 225-250°F (107-121°C) for approxi- mately 15-20 minutes, or until the clams open and are cooked through. The smoky flavor will infuse into the clams, enhancing their natural brininess.

4. Baste with Garlic and Herb Mix: During the last 5 minutes of smoking, generously baste the smoked clams with the prepared garlic and herb mixture.

Serving:

1. Serve Hot: Carefully remove the smoked clams from the smoker.

2. Garnish and Enjoy: Garnish the smoked clams with additional fresh herbs if desired. Serve hot, either as an appetizer or as part of a seafood feast.

These Smoked Clams with Garlic and Herbs offer a delightful twist on traditional clam dishes. The smokiness, along with the garlic and herbs, enhances the natural flavors of the clams, making it a unique and delicious seafood option. Enjoy this dish with crusty bread to soak up the flavorful juices.

Conclusion

In the world of outdoor cooking, there's something truly magical about the art of smoking and grilling. It's a journey that combines tradition, technique, and the joy of savoring incredible flavors with family and friends. Throughout the pages of "Smoke and Sizzle: Mastering the Art of Grilling and Smoking," we've explored the essential knowledge, tech- niques, and mouthwatering recipes that make this culinary adventure so special.

From the sizzle of perfectly grilled steaks to the aromatic smoke of slowly smoked brisket, we've delved into the heart of outdoor cooking. We've learned how to choose the right equipment, select the finest ingredients, and master the art of marinades, rubs, and sauces to elevate our dishes to new heights.

Whether you're a seasoned grill master or just starting your journey, this cookbook has aimed to provide you with the tools and inspiration you need to create unforgettable meals. We've uncovered the secrets of grilling and smoking techniques, explored the world of flavors and ingredients, and offered a wide array of recipes that cater to every palate and occasion. As you continue your culinary adventures, remember that outdoor cooking is not just about the food; it's about the experiences and memories created with each meal. So, gather your loved ones, fire up the grill or smoker, and let the tantalizing aromas and delicious flavors of "Smoke and Sizzle" fill your life.

From classic recipes to bold experiments, from the sizzle of a perfectly seared steak to the gentle waft of aromatic smoke, may your journey into the world of grilling and smoking be filled with sizzle, smoke, and the joy of sharing fantastic meals with those you hold dear.

Thank you for embarking on this flavorful journey with us. Happy grilling and smoking!

Thank You

Dear Valued Reader,

I hope you have enjoyed exploring the delicious world of grilling and smoking with our cookbook. Your feedback is incredibly important to us, and we would be truly grateful if you could take a moment to share your thoughts. Whether it's a favorite recipe that has become a staple at your family gatherings, or insights on how we can further enhance your culinary experience, we would love to hear from you. Your review not only helps us to improve, but also assists fellow cooking enthusiasts in discovering the joys of outdoor cook- ing. Please leave your review on Amazon.com and join our community of passionate grill masters and smokers. Thank you for being an essential part of our journey, and happy grilling and smoking!

Warm regards, Brandee Jankoski and Kevin Glynn

www.ingramcontent.com/pod-product-compliance
Lightning Source LLC
Chambersburg PA
CBHW080837120626
46553CB00009B/2470